CHICAGO
n MapGuides

C000001095

Welco

This o̶   cago to help you
visuali.   ...discussed in this guide, and four pages of
valuable information, handy tips and useful addresses.

Discover Chicago through six districts and six maps

A The Loop
B River North / Gold Coast / Streeterville
C Old Town / Lincoln Park / Lakeview
D Bucktown / Wicker Park / Ukrainian Village
E Greektown / Little Italy / Pilsen /Chinatown
F Kenwood / Hyde Park / Woodlawn

For each district there is a double page of addresses (restaurants – listed in
ascending order of price – cafés, bars and shops), followed by a fold-out map
for the relevant area with the essential places to see (indicated on the map by
a star ★). These places are by no means all that Chicago has to offer, but to us
they are unmissable. The grid-referencing system (**A** B2) makes it easy for you
to pinpoint addresses quickly on the map.

Transportation and hotels in Chicago

The last fold-out consists of a transportation map and four pages of practical
information that include a selection of hotels.   •

Thematic index

Lists all the street names, sites and monuments featured in this guide.

DOWNTOWN FROM MICHIGAN AVENUE BRIDGE

July

Taste of Chicago
→ *Late June-early July in Grant Park; food booths, cookery classes and concerts*
Fourth of July Fireworks
→ *July 3; spectacular fire-works display in Grant Park*
Pitchfork Music Festival
→ *Fri-Sun mid-July, in Union Park; Chicago's largest independent music festival*

August

Bud Billiken Parade
→ *Second Sat, along King Dr. (39th to 51st); the largest African American parade and picnic in the US, named after a fictional character and guardian angel of children*
Lollapalooza
→ *Three days, in Grant Park. Huge music festival; www.lollapalooza.com*

September-October

Mexican Independence Parade
→ *Early Sep, on Columbus Dr.*
Around the Coyote
→ *One weekend mid-Sep celebrating emerging local artists and galleries, in the Wicker Park area; www.aroundthecoyote.org*
Chicago Marathon
→ *Second Sun in Oct; the fastest marathon in the world thanks to the city's flat ground*

November

Mag Mile Lights Festival
→ *Third Sat; more than one million lights hung on Michigan Ave, followed by fireworks by the river*
Thanksgiving Parade
→ *Last Thu; on State St*

December

New Year's Eve Fireworks
→ *Buckingham Fountain*

MONEY MATTERS

Credit cards
They are widely accepted throughout the city. There are ATMs in almost every hotel.

Tax
Taxes are complicated in Chicago and can actually vary depending where you are. Sales tax is about 10 percent, and hotel room taxes more than 15 percent.

Budget

Accommodation
Allow $120–150 a night for a double room in a standard hotel, though booking via an Internet search engine will reduce prices significantly.

Eating out
Fine restaurants can easily top $100 per person, but Mexican restaurants, diners, and fast food cost $5 per person or less.

Going out
Some bars and clubs apply cover charge ($8 to $15).

Tipping
In restaurants 15–20 percent of the bill is appropriate. Taxi drivers expect 10 to 15 percent of the fare; bartenders $1 tip per drink.

ARCHITECTURE

Chicago School (1880–1910)
Following the Fire of 1871, architects like John Root, Louis Sullivan, William Le Barron Jenney, and Dankmar Adler produced masterpieces of brilliant engineering throughout town (**Rookery, Chicago Cultural Center**) and pushed the city's skyline upward (**Monadnock**), eventually leading to the first steel-framed skyscraper in 1885.

Classical Revival, or Beaux-Art (1920)
Chief architect: Daniel Burnham; symmetrical façades; columns, cornices, and pediments; the 1893 Columbian World Exposition, known as the **White City**.

Prairie School (1895–1915)
Chief architect: Frank Lloyd Wright; innovative, mostly residential architecture mixing intricate geometric design with environmental and Eastern elements; **Robie House (F)**; Wright's **Home and Studio** (Oak Park).

International (Modern) style (1930–70)
Ludwig Mies van der Rohe inspired decades of skyscraper building with Bauhaus ideals: cubic shapes, no 'bourgeois' ornamentation, flat roofs, cantilevered construction, metal and glass framework allowing for large windows, sometimes in horizontal bands, and open floor plans; **860-880 Lake Shore Dr.** (1949–51); **111 E. Wacker Dr.** (1970).

CITY PROFILE

■ The Second City or Windy City, as it is also known, is Illinois' largest city and third most populous in the US ■ 2.8 million inhabitants (9.7 million with the suburbs) of whom 37 percent speak a language other than English at home ■ 228 square miles ■ 29 miles of lakefront ■ Average temp.: winter 36F (2C); summer 82F (28C) ■ Chicago is in the Central Standard Time zone, one hour behind New York, six behind London ■ Currency: the US dollar (US$)

NORTH AVENUE BEACH

KEY DATES

1779 Haitian fur trapper Jean Baptiste Pointe du Sable is Chicago's first settler **1837** Chicago founded **1871** Great Chicago Fire **1885** World's first steel-framed skyscraper built **1886** Workers for the eight-hour workday start the Haymarket Riot **1892** The El opens **1893** World's Columbian Exposition **1931** Al Capone finally jailed, for tax evasion **1955** Richard J. 'Boss' Daley elected mayor; remains so until his death in 1976 **1989** His son Richard M. Daley elected mayor (still is)

TOURIST INFO

Visitor Information Centers

→ 163 E Pearson Ave (**B** C4)
→ 77 E Randolph St (**A** B2)
Tel. 1-877-244-2246
Mon-Fri 8am–7pm (6pm Fri);
Sat-Sun 9am (10am Sun)–
6pm; www.cityofchicago.org

WWW.

→ choosechicago.com
The Chicago Convention & Tourism Bureau website.
→ encyclopedia.chicago history.org
The name says it all.
→ www.metromix.com
The Chicago Tribune's site for restaurant, bar, and club reviews, and much more.
→ gochicago.com
→ chicagoreader.com
Music, theater, restaurant listings by local experts.
→ enjoyillinois.com
Website of the Illinois Bureau of Tourism.

TELEPHONE

UK to Chicago

→ 00 + 1 (USA) + 312 (Illinois) + seven-digit number
Chicago to the UK
→ 011 + 44 (UK) + number minus the initial 0
Within the US
→ 1 + three-digit area code + number
Useful numbers
Police or emergency medical service
→ Tel. 911
Directory inquiries
→ Tel. 411 or 555-1212
International operator
→ Tel. 0

DIARY OF EVENTS

Public holidays

Jan 1 (New Year's Day); Third Mon in Jan (Martin Luther King Jr's Birthday); First Mon in March (Pulaski Day; Illinois only); Third Mon in Feb (Presidents' Day); Last Mon in May (Memorial Day); July 4 (Independence Day); First Mon in Sep (Labor Day); Nov 11 (Veterans Day); Fourth Thu in Nov (Thanksgiving); Dec 25 (Christmas Day)

January-February

Chinese New Year Parade
→ Dates vary; www.chicago chinatown.org

March

St Patrick's Day Parade
→ Sat before March 17, in the Loop, the Chicago River is dyed green
South Side Irish St Patrick's Day Parade
→ Sun before March 17, on Western Ave (103rd to 114th); one of the largest Irish parades outside Dublin

April

Chicago Improv Festival
→ Four days late spring–early summer; improv troops at various venues; www.chicago improvfestival.org

May

Bike the Drive
→ Sun before Memorial Day; 15- or 30-mile bike ride along a car-free Lake Shore Dr.; www.bikethedrive.org
Cinco de Mayo
→ First week, in Pilsen; five-day festival celebrating Mexico's 1861 victory over the French
Polish Constitution Day Parade
→ First Sat; celebrates Poland's Constitution Day (May 3, 1791); folk dancing, marching bands, etc.

June

Chicago Blues Festival
→ Four days late May–early June, in Grant Park; the best blues festival in the world
Chicago Gospel Festival
→ First weekend; free concerts in Grant Park
Printers Row Book Fair
→ First weekend; publishers, book dealers, bookbinders and papermakers show their craft on Dearborn St; www.printersrowbookfair.org
Gay & Lesbian Pride Parade
→ Last Sun; Lincoln Park

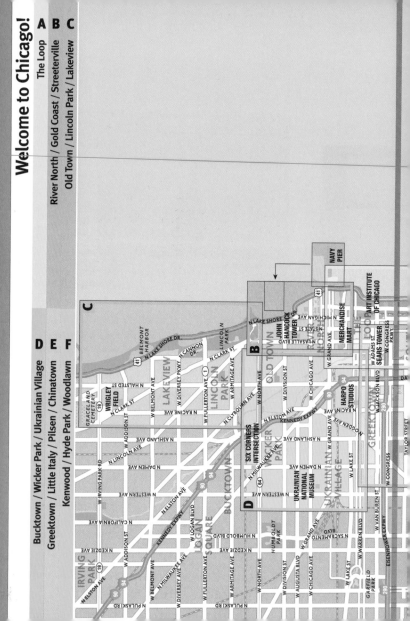

Welcome to Chicago!

A The Loop
B River North / Gold Coast / Streeterville
C Old Town / Lincoln Park / Lakeview
D Bucktown / Wicker Park / Ukrainian Village
E Greektown / Little Italy / Pilsen / Chinatown
F Kenwood / Hyde Park / Woodlawn

LAKE MICHIGAN

MUSEUM CAMPUS

BURNHAM PARK HARBOR

A

SOUTH LOOP

CHINATOWN SQUARE

NEAR SOUTH SIDE

S MICHIGAN AVE
S STATE ST
S CANAL ST
S HALSTED ST

DAN RYAN EXPWY

STEVENSON EXPWY
S INDIANA AVE
S MARTIN LUTHER KING JR DR
S STATE ST
S LASALLE ST
S WENTWORTH AVE
DAN RYAN EXPWY

E 15TH ST
E 31ST ST
E OAKWOOD BLVD
E 43RD ST
E 47TH ST

KENWOOD

PROMONTORY POINT

MUSEUM OF SCIENCE AND TECHNOLOGY

S LAKE SHORE DR

JACKSON PARK

HYDE PARK

E HYDE PARK BLVD
E 55TH ST
S WOODLAWN AVE

UNIVERSITY OF CHICAGO

E 63RD ST

S CORNELL DR
E MARQUETTE DR

BROOKDALE

S STONY ISLAND AVE
E 67TH ST

OAKWOODS CEMETERY

S COTTAGE GROVE AVE

DUSABLE MUSEUM OF AFRICAN AMERICAN HISTORY

WASHINGTON PARK

F

E MARQUETTE RD
S CHICAGO AVE
S CHICAGO SKWY

PARK MANOR

BRIDGEPORT

W 31ST ST
W 35TH ST
W PERSHING RD
W 43RD ST
W 47TH ST
W 51ST ST
W GARFIELD BLVD
W 59TH ST
W 63RD ST
W 71ST ST

S HALSTED ST
S RACINE AVE
S ASHLAND AVE

ENGLEWOOD

S MARQUETTE RD

W CONGRESS PKWY

EISENHOWER EXPWY

LITTLE ITALY

TAYLOR STREET

W ROOSEVELT RD

PILSEN

NATIONAL MUSEUM OF MEXICAN ART

W 18TH ST
W CERMAK RD

LOWER WEST SIDE

E

S DAMEN AVE
S ASHLAND AVE
S DAMEN AVE
S WESTERN AVE

BRIGHTON PARK

GAGE PARK

S WESTERN AVE
W MARQUETTE RD

CHICAGO LAWN

DOUGLAS PARK

W CERMAK RD
W OGDEN AVE

S CALIFORNIA AVE

S SACRAMENTO AVE

S CALIFORNIA AVE

W ROOSEVELT RD
W CERMAK RD
W 26TH ST

STEVENSON EXPWY

S KEDZIE AVE
S KEDZIE AVE

W 35TH ST
W 47TH ST

S ARCHER AVE

W 59TH ST
W 63RD ST

S PULASKI RD

1/11 000 · 1 cm = 1.11 km

0   1   1.25 miles
0   2 km

THE GREAT CHICAGO FIRE

Legend says Catherine O'Leary's cow kicked over a lantern, starting the Fire of 1871. What's known is it started near her house on the Southwest Side. In 36 hours, downtown was destroyed, some 18,000 buildings burned, some 100,000 Chicagoans lost their homes, and at least 300 died. It proved a defining moment for the city. The push to rebuild fueled the birth of the city's ambitious architectural culture and created much of the downtown we see today.

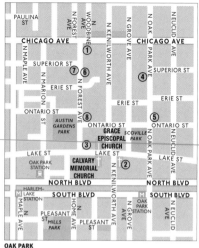

OAK PARK

Lakefront bike path

This amazing 18-mile lakefront bike trail takes you to beautiful beaches, parks, historical locations, countless spectacular views, and numerous tourist attractions. Check www.bikechicago.com for rental addresses, tour suggestions, etc. See also the Hotels page.

SHOPPING

The heart of Chicago's smart retail is the **Magnificent Mile** (see **B**) on N Michigan, extending west on Oak and north on Rush. The city's other major retail strip is **State Street** (see **A**) between Lake and Jackson. These strips include the same stores you'll find in other major American cities. However, for boutique shopping and local independent retailers with more unique

merchandise walk on **W Armitage Ave** (see **C**) and **N Division St / N Milwaukee Ave** (see **D**).

NIGHTLIFE

Where

There's plenty going on any night of the week. With the exception of cultural events at Millennium Park and in the theaters, the Loop quiets down at night.

Lakeview

For the gay club scene of N Halsted and the sporty bar scene on Clark near Addison.

Lincoln Park

During the day, Lincoln Park is full of middle-aged professionals pushing strollers. At night, Clark Street and Lincoln Avenue get swarmed with their rowdy younger counterparts.

Rush Street

This wedge-shaped area bounded by Chicago, Rush,

and State is known as the Viagra Triangle because of its number of singles bar and 'May-December' pickup scene. The draw: restaurants, clubs, and well-heeled patrons.

Wicker Park

The action is along North and Milwaukee, and south on Division; the crowd is an interesting mix: young professionals on the prowl, clubbers out for live music, and foodies looking for a good meal.

Improv comedy

Chicago is the birthplace of improvisation and John Candy, Bill Murray, John Belushi, Mike Myers are just a few of the many prominent alumni. See **C** for the two best addresses.

Cultural listings

→ www.chicagoreader.com Excellent free weekly, with local news, extensive arts coverage, and event listings.

OAK PARK

→ *8 miles west of the Loop; CTA Green Line train to Oak Park Ave*
Chicago's most famous suburb is home to the world's largest collection of houses designed by Frank Lloyd Wright, who lived and worked here from 1889 to 1909. His first home and studio (951 Chicago Ave; **1**) is undoubtedly the main attraction. You can book guided tours of the house and the area here (www.gowright.org; tel. (708) 848-1976), or get a free map from the Oak Park Visitors Center (158 N Forest Ave, www.visitoakpark.com; **3**) if you're content looking from the sidewalk. Another gem is the 1908 Unity Temple, in Wright's own words his 'little jewel' (875 Lake St; **2**). Other highlights include: Frank W. Thomas House (210 N Forest Ave; **8**), Wright's first true Prairie-style house (1901); Arthur Heurtley House (318 N Forest Ave; **6**), whose 1902 design makes way for Robie House; and the early (1895; rebuilt 1923) Tudor-style Nathan Moore House (**7**), an interesting contrast with Wright's later flat-roof constructions. Writer Ernest Hemingway was born in Oak Park. His well-preserved boyhood home (339 N Oak Park Ave; **4**) is worth a visit, as is the nearby Hemingway Museum (200 N Oak Park Ave; tel. (708) 848-2222; **5**).

ONE OF MACY'S CLOCKS

NAVY PIER

THE CHICAGO RIVER

CHICAGO BLUES

In the early 20th century, waves of African American migration brought blues from America's Southern states to Chicago. A powerful urban blues scene emerged in the 1940s and '50s when influential performers such as Muddy Waters, Howlin' Wolf, Otis Rush, and Buddy Guy swapped the acoustic guitar and harmonica of the Delta blues for microphones, drums, and electric guitars in order to be heard in the city's noisy bars. Chicago's identity and the music were soon melded together.

OPENING HOURS

Businesses and banks
→ *Mon-Fri 9am–5pm*
Shops
→ *Mon-Sat 10am–6pm; Sun times vary*
Bars and pubs
→ *Daily 11am–2am to 4am*
Clubs
→ *Daily 9pm–2am*
Restaurants
→ *Usually 7am–10pm; often closed Sun or Mon*
Museums
→ *Usually daily 9am–5pm; the closing day varies*

EATING OUT

Recently *Gourmet Magazine* named Chicago's Alinea (see **C**) the best restaurant in the nation, putting it at the top of the list of the city's gourmet restaurants. However, there are options for every budget – dim sum in Chinatown, Italian on Taylor, Polish on Milwaukee, cutting edge on Randolph, Indian cuisine on Devon, steak houses downtown, or Mexican food in Pilsen, the city's diversity makes eating out a blast.

Dogs...
Chicago has unique takes on both hot dogs and pizza. For a traditional Chicago hot dog, get a dog 'with everything'. Note that ketchup should not be involved! You'll taste Chicago's finest if you buy one from any of the following places: **Gold Coast Dogs** (multiple locations); **Portillo's** (see **B**); **Wiener's Circle** (2622 N Clark St; **C** B4); **Murphy's Red Hots** (1211 W Belmont Ave; **C** A3); and **Hot Doug's** (3324 N California Ave; off **D** A1).

...and slices
Chicago pizza means lots of cheese in a thick crust, with the sauce on top. To go traditional, pick a size and order stuffed spinach. For the best heavy-duty pies, go to: **Giordano's** (multiple locations); **Pizzeria Uno** (29 E Ohio St; **B** B5); **Chicago's** (multiple Locations); and **Edwardo's** (multiple locations).

BEST VIEWS

→ From the Skydeck of the **Sears Tower** (**A**), the highest viewpoint in the city, 1,353 ft above ground.
→ From the middle of **Michigan Avenue Bridge** (**B**).
→ From **Navy Pier** (**B**).
→ From the observatory or bar level of the **John Hancock Center** (**B**).
→ From **North Avenue Beach** (**C**).

CHICAGO ANOTHER WAY

Brown Line
The CTA's Brown Line train has been called the greatest urban theme park ride in the country. Elevated above many small buildings, it offers great views as the train snakes northwest. Turn around and head back to catch a unique glimpse of downtown as the train circles the Loop.

Riverboat architecture tours
The Chicago Architecture Foundation are the best, with knowledgeable guides who hit over 50 sites during the 90-minute cruise up the Chicago River. The CAF also offers excellent walking and bus tours.
→ *224 S Michigan Ave Tel. (312) 922 3432; advance ticket purchase advised; www. architecture.org*

Personal guide
→ *www.chicagogreeter.com* Two- to four-hour insider tours of the city led by enthusiastic volunteers.

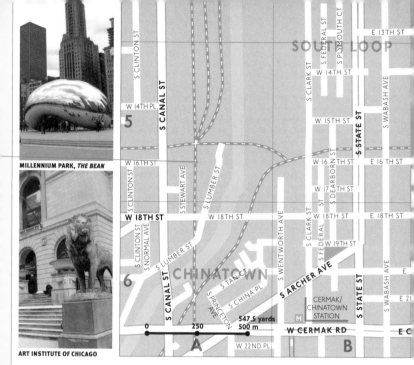

MILLENNIUM PARK, *THE BEAN*

ART INSTITUTE OF CHICAGO

★ Wacker Drive (A B1)
This street begins in the
northeast corner of the Loop
and wraps around the
central business district.
Walk the top level of this
double-decker street to get
a sense of downtown: start
at Michigan and go past the
corncob-esque Marina City
Towers, Merchandise Mart,
the Civic Opera House, the
downtown bridges, and end
at the foot of the Sears Tower.

★ Daley Plaza (A B2)
→ *W Washington St, between
Clark and Dearborn*
A big, ambiguous-faced
1967 Picasso sculpture
anchors this square,
notable for regular public

events, its green market,
and the ring of landmarks
around it: City Hall (west),
the Helmut Jahn-designed
James Thompson Center
(northwest), the Mies van
der Rohe-inspired Daley
Center (north), and Chicago
Temple (south), the world's
tallest church building.

**★ Chicago Cultural
Center (A** B2)
→ *78 E Washington St
Tel. (312) 744-6630; Mon-Fri
8am–7pm (6pm Fri); Sat-Sun
9am (10am Sun)–6pm*
Completed in 1897, this
opulent neoclassical building, with a marble staircase
and two stunning stained-
glass domes, started as the

city's first public library.
Modernized in 1977, and
renamed the Cultural
Center, it is a place to catch
historical and cultural
exhibits, as well as dance,
concerts, and theater.

**★ Art Institute of
Chicago (A** B-C2)
→ *111 S Michigan Ave
Tel. (312) 443-3600; Daily
10.30am–5pm (8pm Thu); free
admission Thu; www.artic.edu*
One of the world's great
museums, whose
Impressionist and
Postimpressionist collection
is considered the most
important outside France.
The newest addition is by
architect Renzo Piano.

★ Millennium Park (A C
→ *201 E Randolph St
Daily 6am–11pm*
This magnificent 24.5-acre
park has many attactions,
but Anish Kapoor's *Cloud
Gate* sculpture (nicknamed
The Bean), the 50-ft faces o
Jaume Plensa's Crown
Fountain, and the grand
arches of the Frank Gehry-
designed band shell are
the local favorites.

**★ LaSalle Financial
Canyon (A** B3)
→ *N LaSalle St, between
Adams and Jackson*
While the mighty Art Deco
Board of Trade Building
(1930) looms over all the
others in the area, the

A

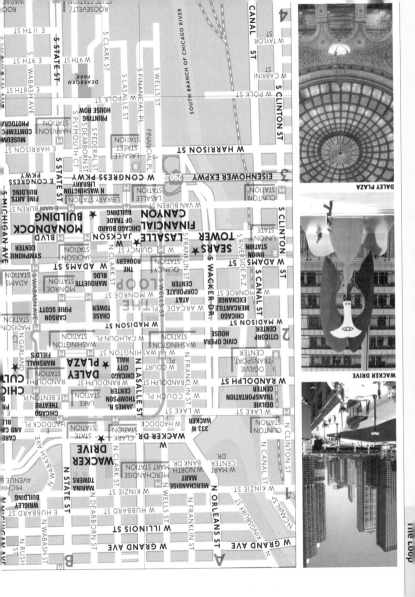

Chicago's central business district takes its name from the public transit rail lines that still clatter in a loop before heading back out into the city's neighborhoods. The area is defined by its strong architectural features: the façades along Michigan Avenue that stare out across Millennium Park toward Lake Michigan, historic gems like the Rookery, and vertical giants like the Monadnock and the Sears Tower, which mark the city as the birthplace of the skyscraper. Here, you can take in a panorama of the city's history, and discover the ambition that drove its growth in the 19th century.

The à la carte prices given in this guide are average prices for a main course only.

17 WEST AT THE BERGHOFF   LOU MITCHELL'S RESTAURAN

RESTAURANTS

17 West at the Berghoff (A B2)
→ 17 W Adams St (State) Tel. (312) 427-3170; Mon-Sat 11am–9pm (10pm Fri-Sat)
A few years ago, the century-old Berghoff got revamped with a new name (17 West), and a more contemporary menu, but thankfully it has kept some of the old German classics (wiener schnitzel, sauerkraut, and bratwurst). If pressed for time, head to the bar to grab a sandwich and a house beer. $12.

Lou Mitchell's Restaurant (A A3)
→ 565 W Jackson Blvd (Clinton); Tel. (312) 939-3111 Daily 5.30am (7am Sun)–3pm
Across from the Sears Tower, on the west bank of the river, this local institution is a great place for a big quintessential American diner breakfast. Fresh-made donuts ease the wait when it's busy, but save room for one of the fluffy omelets. $10.

Eleven City Diner (A B4)
→ 1112 S Wabash Ave (11th) Tel. (312) 212-1112; Mon-Thu 8.30am–9pm (11pm Fri); Fri-Sun 9am–11pm (9pm Sun)
This place quickly became a favorite by offering high-

quality classic deli food. Go for any of the pastrami sandwiches, with a milkshake or egg cream to go with it. Big salads and veggie options too. $10.

The Gage (A B2)
→ 24 S Michigan Ave (Madison); Tel. (312) 372-2979; Daily 11am–midnight; brunch Sat-Sun 10am–2.30pm bar open until 2am (3am Sat)
This handsome gastropub sits across from Millennium Park in one of three Louis Sullivan buildings (1890) and offers rich, smart brasserie food with big global flavors – duck confit, Canadian poutine, Brie fondue. The wine and beer lists give you a wealth of options. $20–30.

Rhapsody (A B2)
→ 65 E Adams St (Wabash) Tel. (312) 786-9911; Mon-Fri 11.30am–2pm, 5–9pm (10pm Thu-Fri); Sat 5–10.30pm; Sun 4.30– 9pm; closed Sun and earlier in summer
It's next to the Symphony Center, so music lovers are a big contingent pre- and post-CSO performances. Delicious seasonal American food by chef Doran Payne, who trained at London's Cordon Bleu and at Taillevent in Paris; gorgeous patio for summer dining. $14 (lunch)–24 (dinner).

RAPSODY

BUDDY GUY'S LEGENDS

MACY'S

Custom House (A B3)
→ 500 S Dearborn (Congress)
Tel. (312) 523-0200; Mon-Fri 11.30am–2pm, 5–10pm; Sat 5–10.30pm; Sun 5–9pm
After star chef Shawn McClain opened highly successful seafood- and vegetable-themed restaurants, he went for the meat. Pork chops with caramelized fennel, braised rabbit with home-made bacon are some of the dishes offered at this modern, comfortable, and hip incarnation of a steak house. For those who don't want meat, the seasonal, daily-changing menu also has plenty of fresh fish options. $26.

Everest (A B3)
→ 440 S LaSalle St (Van Buren); Tel. (312) 663-8920; Tue-Fri 5.30–9pm (9.30pm Fri); Sat 5–10pm
This is an old-world dining room on the 40th floor of the Chicago Stock Exchange, with wonderful views (but book ahead and ask for one of the few tables by the windows), and a high-end menu of French-Alsatian dishes such as pork cheeks with choucroute salad, or sautéed beef with Alsace marrow quenelles. Superb wine list. $30–40.

BAR, NIGHTLIFE

Martini Bar (A B3)
→ 401 S LaSalle St (Van Buren); Tel. (312) 377-6111 Mon-Fri 11am–11pm
With a handsome bar and a black-and-white stone floor, this cocktail lounge is a favorite of traders from the nearby financial center. Get here after 5pm when most of them will have left, and try one of the 37 martinis.

Buddy Guy's Legends (A B3)
→ 754 S Wabash Ave (8th) Tel. (312) 427-1190 Mon-Fri 11am–2am; Sat 5pm–3am; Sun 6pm–2am www.buddyguys.com
Buddy Guy is one of the most influential blues guitarists ever and his well-run club is among the best in the nation. Fans shuddered when it threatened to close, but it's staying put for now. Guy plays there in January, which is not to be missed.

SHOPPING

Macy's (A B2)
→ 111 N State St (Washington) Tel. (312) 781-1000; Mon-Sat 10am–8pm; Sun 11am–6pm
Once the flagship location for Marshall Field's, it is famous for the 7-ton green ornate clocks hanging at two corners of the building and for its mosaic dome – the largest unbroken example of Tiffany glass in the world. The beautiful granite structure has nine floors of furniture, housewares, clothes, cosmetics, toys, and much more. If hungry, head to the seventh-floor food court for a Mexican treat at Frontera Fresco, a branch of Chicago's star chef Rick Bayless (see also **B**).

State Street (A B2)
→ Between Randolph and Jackson
South of Macy's you'll find a thick corridor of name-brand retail that's only overshadowed by the Mag Mile. A little more laid back than its northern counterpart, it's a favorite of Chicagoans, especially during the holidays. It is especially good for bargain hunting: **Filene's Basement** (1 N State St); **T.J. Maxx** (11 N State St); **H&M** (22 N State St); **Loehmann's** department store (151 N State St); **Urban Outfitters** (20 S State St), and **Forever 21** (22 N State St).

Gallery 37 (A B2)
→ 66 E Randolph St (Garland); Tel. (312) 744-7274 Mon-Fri 10am–6pm; Sat 11am–5pm
The city runs a program for public school kids ages 14–21 who apprentice with local artists in various disciplines, whether visual, performing, culinary, or media arts. You can see and buy their work here.

Chicago Architecture Foundation Store (A B2)
→ 224 S Michigan Ave (Adams); Tel. (312) 922-3432 Daily 9am–6.30pm; www.architecture.org
Great gifts in the image of Chicago architecture: everything from Louis Sullivan picture frames, to Frank Lloyd Wright coasters, to dueling busts of Mies van der Rohe and Daniel Burnham.

Iwan Reis (A B2)
→ 19 S Wabash Ave (Madison), 2nd floor Tel. (312) 372-1306 Mon-Sat 9am–5.30pm (5pm Sat)
This fantastic third-generation, family-owned tobacco shop is perched on the second floor of a historic building designed by the famous Adler & Sullivan architecture firm. Even if you don't smoke, the walls of cigars, pipes, and a 5-ft wooden elf are sights to behold.

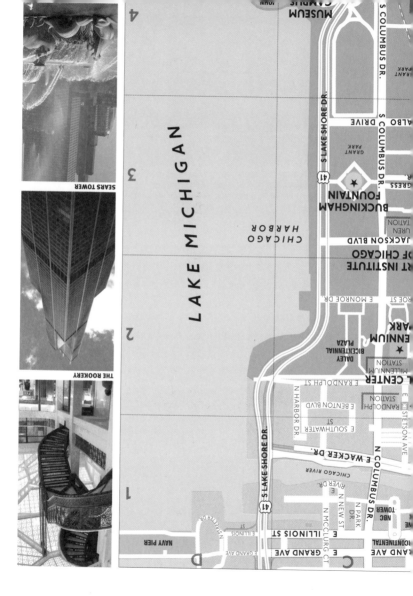

SEARS TOWER

THE ROOKERY

NAVY PIER

LAKE MICHIGAN

CHICAGO
HARBOR

MUSEUM

S COLUMBUS DR.

S COLUMBUS DR.

S LAKE SHORE DR.

GRANT
PARK

ALBO
DRIVE

GRANT
PARK

GRESS

BUCKINGHAM
FOUNTAIN

JACKSON BLVD

OF CHICAGO

RT INSTITUTE

ROE ST

E MONROE DR

URS
TATION

UREN
TATION

ENNIUM
PARK

DALEY
BICENTENNIAL
PLAZA

MILLENNIUM
STATION

L CENTER

E RANDOLPH ST

MILLENNIUM
STATION

RANDOLPH
STATION

STETSON AVE

E RANDOLPH ST

E BENTON BLVD

N HARBOR DR

E SOUTHWATER
ST

E WACKER DR.

N COLUMBUS DR.

S LAKE SHORE DR.

CHICAGO RIVER

E
RIVER DR

NBC
TOWER

NE

N NEW ST

N PARK
DR.

N MCCLURG CT

S LAKE SHORE DR

E GRAND AVE

ILLINOIS ST
E ILLINOIS ST

N STETSON DR

AND AVE

E GRAND AVE

NCONTINENTAL

MONADNOCK

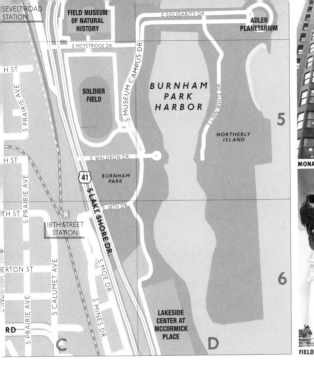

Map labels:
SEVELT ROAD STATION
FIELD MUSEUM OF NATURAL HISTORY
E SOLIDARITY DR
ADLER PLANETARIUM
E MCFETRIDGE DR
SOLDIER FIELD
S MUSEUM CAMPUS DR
BURNHAM PARK HARBOR
S LINN WHITE DR
H ST
S PRAIRIE AVE
5
NORTHERLY ISLAND
E WALDRON DR
41
BURNHAM PARK
H ST
S PRAIRIE AVE
E 18TH DR
S LAKE SHORE DR.
18TH STREET STATION
ERTON ST
S CALUMET AVE
S MOE DR.
6
S PRAIRIE AVE
RD
S MINES DR.
LAKESIDE CENTER AT MCCORMICK PLACE
C
D

FIELD MUSEUM

-story Rookery (1888) is
guably the real jewel. Its
ylight-covered staircase –
signed by Louis Sullivan
d redone in 1906 by Frank
yd Wright, is part of one
the most stunning
teriors in the city.

Sears Tower (A A3)
233 S Wacker Dr.
. (312) 875-9696; Skydeck:
ily 10am–10pm (8pm Oct-
arch); tours available
ter the John Hancock
nter (**B**), architect Bruce
aham and engineer Fazlur
an designed what, for a
arter of a century, was the
rld's tallest building.
mpleted in 1973, it stands
1,450 ft and remains the

peak of Chicago's skyline.

★ **Buckingham
Fountain (A** C3)
Modeled by Edward Bennett
after the Latona Basin at
Versailles, this 280-ft-wide
pink marble giant was
built in 1927, and references
Lake Michigan, with four
seahorses symbolizing
the four states surrounding
it: Wisconsin, Illinois,
Indiana, and Michigan.
It stands in the vast,
319-acre Grant Park, often
referred to as the city's
'front yard'.

★ **Monadnock
Building (A** B3)
→ 53 W Jackson Blvd
Sometimes called the

world's first skyscraper
because when it was
completed in 1891, it was
the world's tallest office
building. Six-ft-thick brick
walls support the massive
structure, whose 16th and
last floor is made entirely
of stone.

★ **Museum Campus (A** C4)
→ 1200–1400 S Lake
Shore Dr.; Daily 9am–5pm;
later in summer
This 57-acre lakefront park
is home to a trifecta of
world-class museums:
John G. Shedd Aquarium
→ Tel. (312) 939-2438
www.sheddaquarium.org
The world's largest indoor
aquarium with some

8,000-plus species.
Don't miss the whales
and dolphins performing
in the Oceanarium and
the sharks of the Wild Reef
wing, which re-creates a
coral reef in the Philippines.
Field Museum
→ Tel. (312) 922-9410
www.fieldmuseum.org
Built for the World's
Columbian Exposition in
1893, this vast science
museum is home to the
world's largest T. rex fossil.
Adler Planetarium
→ Tel. (312) 922-7827
www.adlerplanetarium.org
A pair of stunning theaters
and a playground of
astronomical exhibits.

TRIBUNE TOWER

NAVY PIER

★ Merchandise Mart (B A6)

→ 222 Merchandise Mart Plaza; Tours available, call (312) 527-7762; Shops: Mon-Fri 9am–6pm; Sat 10am–3pm

Built as a wholesale center in 1930, it was the largest building in the world until the Pentagon 11 years later. Today this 25-story Art Deco fortress of retail is mainly occupied by private showrooms and wholesale merchants, but a mall on the first two floors is open to the public.

★ Michigan Avenue Bridge (B C6)

→ Chicago River at E Wacker Dr.

To look into the heart of

Chicago, go here. Towering all around you is the city's architectural muscle. The Mag Mile spreads north between the Wrigley and the Tribune buildings. To the south, Michigan Avenue cuts across the façades that face Millennium Park. To the east, Lake Michigan fades into the Chicago River, which drifts under your feet and toward the city's lattice of moving bridges.

★ Magnificent Mile (B C4-5)

→ 300–900 N Michigan Ave

In the early 20th century city planners hoped to transform what was once a frontier trading post

into a major shopping strip. Gradually the avenue was built up and, in 1947, nicknamed the Magnificent Mile, or Mag Mile.

★ Tribune Tower (B C5)

→ 435 N Michigan Ave

This neo-Gothic tower (1925, John Howell and Raymond Hood) with spires and flying buttresses houses the *Chicago Tribune*. Don't miss rocks from the Parthenon, the Alamo, etc., embedded in the outer wall.

★ Navy Pier (B D5)

→ 600 E Grand Ave

Mon-Sat 10am–8pm (10pm Fri-Sat; 7pm Sun); extended in summer; www.navypier.com

Built in 1916, it's gone from

freight and passenger terminal to naval training base, to university use, to tourist magnet, eventually becoming one of the top attractions in the state. The giant Ferris wheel, tour boats, Smith Museum of Stained Glass, Children's Museum, and grand ballroom are only some of the highlights. Great views of the city, too.

★ John Hancock Center (B C4)

→ 875 N Michigan Ave Observatory: Tel. (312) 751-3681; Daily 9am–11pm

Designed to be a city within a city, this 1,127-ft-high steel-and-black aluminium giant was controversial

B

MERCHANDISE MART

MICHIGAN AVENUE BRIDGE

B

FRANKLIN STATUE

W LASALLE DR.

LINCOLN MONUMENT

CHICAGO HISTORY MUSEUM

ARCHBISHOP'S RESIDENCE

N LAKESHORE DR

ASTOR STREET

★ 1500

N ASTOR ST

N STATE PKWY

E NORTH BLVD

W NORTH BLVD

64 W NORTH AVE

OLD TOWN

W BURTON PL

N DEARBORN PKWY

N CLARK ST

N SANDBURG TER

N LASALLE BLVD

N WELLS ST

N WIELAND ST

N NORTH PARK AVE

N ORLEANS ST

W EUGENIE ST

W CONCORD PL

W CONCORD LN

N WELLS ST

1444

N ASTOR ST

1365

E SCHILLER ST

W SCHILLER ST

N STATE PKWY

N DEARBORN PKWY

N SUTTON PL

N CLARK ST

N SANDBURG TER

N LASALLE BLVD

N WELLS ST

W SCHILLER ST

E BANKS ST

E GOETHE ST

W GOETHE ST

N GOETHE ST

W SCOTT ST

E SCOTT ST

N ASTOR ST

N STATE PKWY

N STONE ST

1200

E DIVISION ST

W DIVISION ST

CLARK/DIVISION STATION

W EVERGREEN AVE

SEWARD PARK

E ELM ST

W ELM ST

N CLARK ST

E CEDAR ST

E BELLEVUE

N RUSH ST

W MAPLE ST

W ELM ST

W HILL ST

W WENDELL ST

W OAK ST

W WALTON ST

N WELLS ST

N ORLEANS ST

GOLD

E RUSH ST

E OAK ST

E WALTON ST

MAG

E DELAWA

PP

E PEARSON

NEWBERRY LIBRARY ★

WASHINGTON SQUARE

N STATE ST

N DEARBORN ST

N LASALLE BLVD

W CHESTNUT ST

N CLARK ST

W LOCUST ST

W WALTON ST

W OAK ST

W CHESTNUT ST

W LOCUST ST

CHICAGO STATION M

CHICAGO STATION M

W INSTITUTE PL

4

W CHICAGO AVE

3

2

1

A

North of the Chicago River, downtown gives way to what's long been some of the city's prime real estate. The area is anchored by the Magnificent Mile on North Michigan Avenue, the city's high-end shopping district, which doubles as home to many of the city's most luxurious hotels. To the east, a forest of high-rises in Streeterville leads back toward the lake and Navy Pier. West of the Mag Mile, the glitz tapers off into the rehabbed warehouses of River North, and the Gallery District. North of Chicago Avenue, tributaries of expensive retail give way to the Gold Coast and Old Town, two residential neighborhoods that both boast pockets full of historic homes.

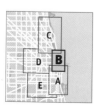

PORTILLO'S

TOPOLOBAMPO

RESTAURANTS

Portillo's (B B5)
→ 100 W Ontario St (Clark)
Daily 10am–11pm
Dick Portillo, who started in 1963 with one small hot-dog stand, now has 45 playfully themed restaurants. The dogs are recommended, but the burgers and Italian beef sandwiches are also great. $2.50.

Café Iberico (B A4)
→ 739 LaSalle Dr. (Superior)
Tel. (312) 573-1510; Mon-Fri 11am–11.30pm (1am Fri); Sat-Sun noon–1.30am (11pm Sun)
This family-friendly tapas bar can involve a long wait but is worth it, if only for the plate of Spanish-style sausages (chorizo y morcilla), the sangria, and the chocolate custard with caramel. Tapas around $5.

RL (B B4)
→ 115 E Chicago (Michigan)
Tel. (312) 475-1100; Daily 11.30am–10pm (11pm Fri-Sat); Sun brunch until 5pm
This Ralph Lauren restaurant – think New York Rhinelander Mansion shop – is a power lunch spot. On the menu, great basics such as steaks, chops, seafood, salads, and BLTs. $15–$25.

Table Fifty-Two (B B3)
→ 52 W Elm St (Dearborn)

Tel. (312) 573-4000
Tue-Sun 11am–2.30pm, 5 (4pm Sun)–10.30pm
A favorite with everyone, this tiny cottage with a stone bar and copper ceiling is helmed by Oprah's former chef Art Smith. The Southern menu includes pistachio-crusted chicken breast and chili-braised pork. Reserve well ahead. $25.

**Frontera Grill /
Topolobampo (B** B5)
→ 445 N Clark St (Hubbard)
Tel. (312) 661-1434; Tue-Sat, lunch and dinner (closed Sat lunch at Topolobampo)
Star chef Rick Bayless uses organic ingredients for his celebrated Mexican cuisine in both colorful, lively restaurants. Try Frontera's tacos al carbon – wood-grilled fish or meat served with salsa, guacamole, and fresh tortillas. The slightly fancier sister restaurant has more elaborate fare: grilled lobster with smoky garlic mojo or shrimp with lime dressing (reservations advised). $15/$30.

Gibson's (B B3)
→ 1028 N Rush St (Bellevue)
Tel. (312) 266-8999
Daily 11am–midnight
This classic-looking steak house, with wood floors and red leather banquettes, serves aged beef cooked to

 ILLY GOAT TAVERN

LUX BAR

JAZZ RECORD MART

order, in generous portions. Ribeyes and New York sirloin are the cuts of choice. The desserts are delicious. Very good wine list. $35.

mk (B A4)
→ 868 N Franklin St (Chestnut)
Tel. (312) 482-9179; Daily 5.30–10pm (11pm Fri-Sat)
This modern, spacious two-story space with a skylight in a vaulted wood ceiling is the perfect setting for chef Erick Simmons' American-French cuisine – soup of pureed artichoke with mussels and jicama, yellowfin tuna with shiitake mushrooms. Extensive wine list. $35.

NoMI (B B4)
→ 800 N Michigan Ave (Chicago), Park Hyatt, 7th fl. Tel. (312) 239-4030; Daily 6.30 (7am Sat-Sun)–10.30am, 11.30am–2.30pm, 5.30–10pm
Find a table near the floor-to-ceiling windows for a breathtaking view of the city, in a modern space lit by Dale Chihuly's unusual glass chandeliers. Japan meets France in chef Christophe David's imaginative dishes; in warm weather, try eating on the garden terrace. $38; breakfast $25.

TRU (B C5)
→ 676 N St Clair St (Erie)

Tel. (312) 202-0001; Mon-Thu 5.30–10pm; Fri-Sat 5–11pm
The double star-power of chef Rick Tramonto and pastry chef Gale Gand is behind this spot, with blue velvet banquettes and cream walls hung with modern art. Try the grilled scallops with chorizo and avocado dumplings or the butter-poached Maine lobster with asparagus. And don't miss Gale's hot chocolate soufflé. The wine list boasts over 1,700 labels. Jacket required. Three-course menu: $95.

CAFÉ, BARS

Fox & Obel Café (B D5)
→ 401 E Illinois St; Tel. (312) 379-0112; Mon-Fri 7am–9pm; varies with seasons
A fantastic grocery store, with a café attached that serves up amazing soups, cold or hot sandwiches, omelets, and dishes such as BBQ baby back ribs or sesame-baked tuna. The cinnamon swirls are dynamite, and so is the coffee.

Billy Goat (B C5)
→ 430 N Michigan Ave, lower level; Tel. (312) 222-1525 Daily 6am–2am
This iconic tavern, long located near the offices of the city's daily newspapers, is still known as a hangout

for reporters and columnists. It is also famous for its 'cheezborgers'.

Lux Bar (B B3)
→ 18 E Bellevue Pl. (Rush) Tel. (312) 642-3400
Mon-Thu 11am–2am; Fri-Sun 8am–2am (3am Sat); kitchen open until midnight
Think Adolph Loos and Vienna for its stylish look; sit at the long bar and order one of the cocktails with the Gold Coast sliders mini-filets – a treat.

The Signature Lounge (B C4)
→ 875 N Michigan Ave, John Hancock Center Tel. (312) 787 7230; Daily 11am–12.30am (1am Fri-Sat)
Take in a dramatic view of Chicago from the tower's 96th floor, with a My o Mai Tai or Signature martini.

SHOPPING

Gallery District (B A4-5)
→ W Chicago Ave (north); W Ontario St (south); N Wells St (east); N Orleans St (west)
This former warehouse district is now home to the city's largest concentration of art galleries: **Albano, Zolla/Lieberman, Stephen Daiter,** and **Alan Koppel Gallery** among others.

Jazz Record Mart (B B5)
→ 27 E Illinois (Wabash) Tel. (312) 222-1467; Mon-Sat

10am–8pm; Sun noon–7pm
Bob Koester, the man behind this shop, is an encyclopedia of jazz and blues history and an independent record label owner (Delmark Records).

Magnificent Mile (B C3-6)
→ 300–900 N Michigan Ave
Lined with historical architectural gems the Mag Mile is also the city's high-end shopping destination with more than 450 stores: Bloomingdale's, Neiman Marcus, Bottega Veneto, Chanel, Vuitton, Saks, Jacadi, and Ralph Lauren, among many others.

Oak Street (B A-B3)
→ Oak St, west of Michigan
Spilling off the Mag Mile is a tributary of smaller upscale shops – Dennis Basso, J. Mendel, Jimmy Choo, Hermes, Kate Spade, Barneys, and jewelers Graff and Harry Winston.

Hidden Treasures (B B4)
→ 46 E Chicago Ave (Wabash); Tel. (312) 943-7761 Mon-Sat 10am–6pm
It really is hidden, next to a Jimmy John's in a second-floor spot off Michigan Avenue. But Northwestern Memorial Hospital's thrift store is an unknown trove; vintage Yves Saint-Laurent, Ralph Lauren couture, and Christian Dior can be had for under $50.

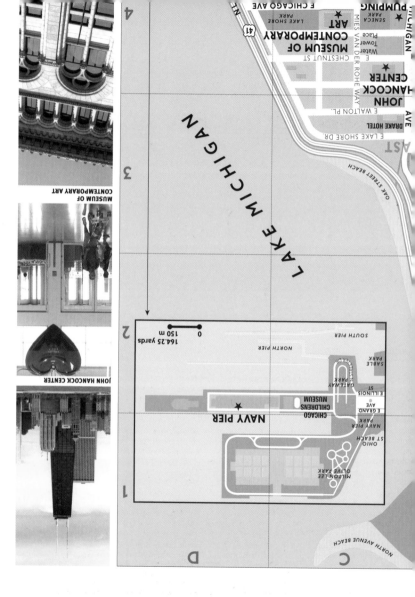

WATER TOWER

ASTOR STREET

hen it was completed in 969. If traveling without children, skip the bservatory and its open-air iewing deck on the 94th oor and go to the bar two oors up, where views are ust as staggering.

★ Museum of ontemporary Art (B C4)
➜ *220 E Chicago Ave el. (312) 280-2660 ue-Sun 10am–5pm (8pm ue); www.mcachicago.org* his austere four-story uilding, designed by Berlin rchitect Josef Paul Kleihues n 1997, has a superb ollection – so vast only fraction is shown at any ne time – of works by Magritte, Calder, Sol LeWitt,

Cindy Sherman, Jeff Koons, Richard Long, among many others.

★ Newberry Library (B B3)
➜ *60 W Walton St Tel. (312) 943-9090; Tue-Thu 10am–6pm; Fri-Sat 9am–5pm*
In 1887 Chicago business-man Walter Loomis Newberry made this stately building home to one of the largest private libraries in the world, with an impressive array of maps, books, and manuscripts focused on Western Europe and the Americas.

★ Water Tower and Pumping Station (B C4)
➜ *806 and 811 N Michigan Ave*
Following the 1871 Chicago

Fire, the tower (1869) and pumping station (1866), saved by their stone walls, stood virtually alone among the ashes in this area of the city. Since then, they have survived disparaging remarks by Oscar Wilde, who called the tower a monstrosity, and have been saved three times from demolition by public outcry. Two of a few remaining structures by William W. Boyington, one of Chicago's prominent early architects.

★ Astor Street (B B1-2)
➜ *Between E Division St and E North Blvd*
A virtual parade of beautiful residential architecture, this stretch has more than two

dozen historic buildings – many dating back to the late 1800s. At 1365 N Astor, the low, brick-and-limestone Charnley-Persky House (1892) is an example of early Frank Lloyd Wright, when he was still working for Louis Sullivan, and typical of his Prairie School style. 1200 N Astor is what some architects say is 'perhaps the ultimate Chicago School apartment building', while at no. 1444 is the Gold Coast's best example of Art Deco: the Edward P. Russell House (1929). Still in the area, at 1340 N State, is Hugh Hefner's original Playboy Mansion.

PEGGY NOTEBAERT NATURE MUSEUM

BOYSTOWN

W WRIGHTWOOD AVE — ST CLEMENT'S — W WRIGHT
W DEMING P
JONQUIL PARK — W DRAPER ST — W LILL AVE — APOLLO THEATER — W LILL AVE
W ALTGELD ST — W ALTGELD ST — W ARLINGTO
W MONTANA ST — FULLERTON STATION
N SOUTHPORT — N RACINE AVE — N SEMINARY AVE — N HALSTED — N BURLING — N ORCHARD ST

W FULLERTON AVE

W FULLERTON

DEPAUL UNIVERSITY CONCERT HALL — CHILDREN'S MEM HOSPITAL — W KEMPER PL.

N SOUTHPORT AVE — N WAYNE AVE — N LAKEWOOD AVE — N MAGNOLIA AVE — N RACINE AVE — N CLIFTON AVE — N SEMINARY AVE — N KENMORE AVE — N SHEFFIELD ST

W BELDEN AVE — **LINCOLN PARK** — VICTORY GARDENS GREENHOUSE THEATRE — LIN PA HOS

W WEBSTER AVE — N BISSELL ST — N FREMONT ST — N DAYTON ST — N HALSTED ST — OZ PARK

5

N CLYBOURN AVE — W DICKENS AVE — N BURLING — W DIC

N KINGSBURY ST — ARMITAGE STATION

W ARMITAGE AVE

W ARMITAGE A

N LARRABEE ST — N BURLING ST — N ORCHARD ST — N HOWE ST

W CORTLAND ST — N MAUD AVE — N SEMINARY AVE — N KENMORE — N SHEFFIELD ST — N BISSELL ST — N DAYTON ST — W WISCONSIN ST — N HALSTED ST

CHICAGO RIVER NORTH BRANCH — N CLYBOURN AVE — MEN

6

W WABANSIA AVE — N THROOP ST — N ADA ST — N KINGSBURY ST — N MARCEY ST — W WILLOW ST — W WILLOW ST — N VINE ST — N LARRABEE ST — N LARRA

NORTHALSTE — N NELSON AVE — STEPPENWOLF THEATRE COMPANY — W CONCORD PL. — ROYAL GEORGE THEATRE

W NORTH AVE

NORTH-CLYBOURN STATION — NORTH-CLYBOURN STATION

A — **B**

C

★ **Lincoln Park** (**C** C5)
Named shortly after President Lincoln was assassinated in 1865, this expanse of greenery started life as a cemetery. By 1875, most of the bodies had been moved, and between then and 1957 the 6-mile-long, 1,200-acre park was being landscaped. It is home to one of the last free zoos in the US.

★ **Chicago History Museum** (**C** C6)
→ 1601 N Clark St
Tel. (312) 642-4600; Mon-Sat 9.30am–4.30pm (8pm Thu); Sun noon–5pm; www.chicago history.org
Did you know that the zipper, the Ferris wheel,

roller skates, and spray paint were invented in Chicago? The museum's millions of artifacts are grouped within eight collections (decorative and industrial arts, costume, oral history, etc.) and include the bed President Abraham Lincoln died in, and one of the nation's largest collections of architectural documents.

★ **Abraham Lincoln Monument** (**C** D6)
→ Lincoln Park (W LaSalle)
Considered by many to be Augustus Saint-Gaudens' most important work, this 1887 bronze depiction of Lincoln freezes him as he stands from a chair to

speak – in a moment that seems surprisingly personal for a formal monument.

★ **Lincoln Park Zoo** (**C** C5)
→ 2001 N Clark St; Tel. (312) 742-2000; Grounds: daily 9am–6pm; buildings and farm 10am–5pm; times vary so call ahead; www.lpzoo.org
It started with the donation of 2 swans from New York's Central Park in 1868, and today is home to more than 1,200 animals and 230 species. Highlights include a huge, state-of-the art habitat for apes and the Pritzker Zoo for children, where they walk through 3 acres of woods and observe red wolves, otters, and bears. Don't miss the

recently restored historic lily pond at the north end

★ **Peggy Notebaert Natu Museum** (**C** C5)
→ 2430 N Cannon Dr.
Tel. (773) 755-5100
Mon-Fri 9am–4.30pm; Sat-Sun 10am– 5pm; www. naturemuseum.org
Opened in 1999, the museum is interactive, designed to teach childre about nature – from the li of a river to sounds of wilc animals. The butterfly haven, with more than 75 different species, is a mus

★ **North Avenue Beach** (**C** D6)
→ North Ave at the lake
From the north to the sou end of the city, Chicago is

ABRAHAM LINCOLN MONUMENT

CHICAGO HISTORY MUSEUM

Heading north, pass through three residential neighborhoods that embody different waves of gentrification. While the Gold Coast was almost always home to the affluent, Old Town was once home to immigrant German laborers. One of the nation's first neighborhood revitalization movements made it highly desirable, but you can still find quiet streets of modest-sized homes. Farther north, you'll come upon Lincoln Park, populated by young professionals, brash new condominiums, and lively bars. At the north end of Lincoln Park, Lakeview is more of a mix – with the free-spirited Boystown, the sporty orbit of Wrigleyville, and some punky swagger near Clark and Belmont.

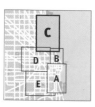

PICK ME UP

ALINEA

RESTAURANTS

Chicago Diner (C B2)
→ 3411 N Halsted St (Roscoe)
Tel. (773) 935-6696; Daily
11am (10am Sat-Sun)–10pm;
extended hours in summer
It caters to vegans and raw-food diners, has been collecting awards for best vegetarian restaurant for 25 years, and even meat eaters rave about the Reuben sandwich. Organic beers and vegan shakes. $9.

Pick Me Up (C A2)
→ 3408 N Clark St (Roscoe)
Tel. (773) 248-6613; Mon-Thu
11am–3am; nonstop from
11am Fri until 5am Sun
A great late-night option is this funky diner south of Wrigley Field. In a relaxed atmosphere, you'll get a delicious and surprisingly vegetarian-friendly menu. $9.

Zad (C B3)
→ 3112 N Broadway (Briar)
Tel. (773) 404-3473
Daily 11am–10pm
Though modest-looking, this small Middle Eastern spot offers many of the standards – shawarma, hummus, baba ganoush – but a little extra care sets it apart. $11.

Tango Sur (C A2)
→ 3763 N Southport Ave
(Grace); Tel. (773) 477-5466
Mon-Sat 5–10.30pm (11.30pm
Fri-Sat); Sun noon–11pm
The best time to hit this fabulous Argentinian steak house is during the week, as weekend waits can be long. Bring your own wine to accompany perfectly cooked, free-range, grass-fed Argentian beef at very reasonable prices. $18.

North Pond (C C4)
→ 2610 N Cannon Dr.
(Fullerton); Tel. (773) 477-5845
Tue-Sun 11.30am–1.30pm,
5.30–10pm; closed Sat lunch,
and Tue in Jan-April
This former ice-skaters' shelter turned topflight restaurant is at the edge of a pond overlooking the skyline. Try the ribeye à la plancha with polenta or eggs with morels and fava beans; whenever possible, chef Bruce Sherman uses seasonal ingredients from small local farms. $35.

Charlie Trotter's (C B5)
→ 816 W Armitage (Halsted)
Tel. (773) 248-6228
Tue-Sat seatings at 6pm
(5.30pm Fri) and 9pm
Charlie Trotter is the patriarch of the city's elite chefs. Quail with chorizo, spring onions and clover, and artichoke soup with spearmint and honey are examples of the dishes on offer. Call well ahead – your taste buds will thank you

BOURGEOIS PIG

BITTERSWEET

OLD TOWN ALE HOUSE

for your effort and planning. Jackets required. Grand menu $200; Vegetable menu $125.

Alinea (C B6)
→ *1723 N Halsted (Willow) Tel. (312) 867-0110; Daily 5.30 (5 Sat-Sun)–9.30pm* Chef-owner Grant Achatz and his team offer a 'tasting' menu of 13 (bite-size) courses, and a more extensive 28-course 'tour' menu, both of which include aesthetically dazzling lineups of brilliant dishes. Menus $145 and $225.

CAFÉS, BARS, MUSIC

Bourgeois Pig (C B5)
→ *738 W Fullerton Pkwy (Burling); Tel. (773) 929-6570 Daily 7am (8am Sun)–11pm* This two-story cozy, old-fashioned Lincoln Park café serves amazing, freshly made sandwiches, salads, and daily baked desserts; outdoor tables in warm weather.

Bittersweet (C A3)
→ *1114 W Belmont Ave (Clifton); Tel. (773) 929-1100 Tue-Fri 7am–7pm; Sat-Sun 8am–7pm (6pm Sun)* Grab a seat at one of the marble tables for the pastries that set the place apart. Cheesecakes, pies, tarts, cookies, and

cobblers will delight those with a sweet tooth.

Old Town Ale House (C C6)
→ *219 W North Ave (Wells) Tel. (312) 944-7020; Mon-Sat 8am–4am; Sun noon–4am* A dive bar of the finest variety, with a wealth of character. The owner's artwork decorates the walls – portraits of famous Chicagoans and lewd scenes not for the meek. A fine jukebox plays jazz and soul records.

Minibar | Winebar (C B3)
→ *3339 / 3341 N Halsted St (Buckingham) Tel. (773) 871-6227 Minibar: Mon-Fri 7pm–2am Sat-Sun 5pm–3am (2am Sun). Winebar: daily 5pm– midnight (2am Fri-Sat); brunch Sat-Sun 11am–3pm* Winebar has a good list of wines, and substantial food; Minibar is a classy cocktail lounge with live DJs some nights. On weekends tables get cleared away after 11pm and the party takes over both spaces.

Green Mill Cocktail Lounge (C off A1)
→ *4802 N Broadway St Tel. (773) 878 5552 Daily noon–4am (5am Sat)* Once a hangout of Al Capone, there are still escape tunnels from when

his gang ran a speakeasy here. Today it's known for its legendary late-night jam sessions and Sunday night poetry slams.

SHOPPING

Armitage Ave (C A-C5-6)
→ *Between Racine & Halsted* A Mecca for boutique shoppers, it is cluttered with the city's best women's shops and spas. At **SHE Boutique** (no.1024, [773] 880-8061), a mix of high/low contemporary and evening-wear by Rebecca Taylor, Karta, and Love by Yaya hangs from industrial chains. Next door at **Entendre Couture** (no. 1022A, [773] 248-1022) owner Dina Mansur's Siberian husky charms visitors as they peruse racks of Tag, Raven Denim, and Chip & Pepper – the city's best jeans selection. Nonfashion stores include **Paper Source** (no. 919, [773] 525-7300), a terrific card and stationery shop, and **Vosges Haut-Chocolat** (no. 951; [773] 296-9866), where Paris-trained Katrina Markoff makes chocolate with everything: hot chiles, candied violet, tangy curry powder, and even salty bacon.

Uncle Fun (C A3)
→ *1338 W Belmont Ave (Southport) Tel. (773) 477-8223 Tue-Fri noon–7pm; Sat-Sun 11am–7pm (5pm Sun)* A spectacular old-school toy store stuffed with bins, odd items, good and bad pranks, and classic gags.

THEATERS

The Second City (C C6)
→ *1616 N Wells St (North) Tel. (312) 337-3992 (box office); www.secondcity.com* This theater has launched quite a few comedy careers over the past 50 years – including those of Mike Myers, Bill Murray, and John Belushi. Each of the two stages has a resident crew of performers, who create and perform original skit-based shows.

IO (formerly Improv Olympic) (C A2)
→ *3541 N Clark St (Eddy) Tel. (773) 880-0199 (box office); www.ioimprov.com* Another pillar of the city's influential comedy scene, it was the Improv Olympic until the Olympic Committee threatened a lawsuit. Here performers craft entire shows on the fly. The results range from groaningly mediocre to mind-boggling brilliant.

NORTH AVENUE BEACH

OLD TOWN TRIANGLE DISTRICT

ELKS VETERANS ★
MEMORIAL

DIVERSEY
LAGOON

VIEW AVE
N DR.

DIVERSEY DR.

ST. JOSEPH ✚
HOSPITAL

COMMONWEALTH AVE

N
AVE

N. SHERIDAN RD

N. LAKE SHORE DR.

N. LAKE SHORE DR. W.

AVE

RRY
PL.

ON

AVE

BELMONT
HARBOR

VE

ST

E

N. HARBOR DR

BIRD
SANCTUARY

DR

LAKE MICHIGAN

1   2   3   4

D   C

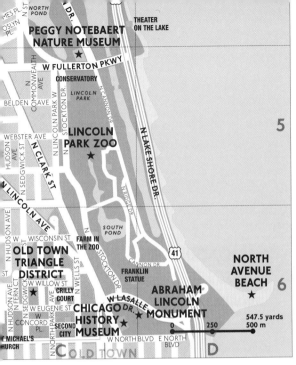

THEATER
ON THE LAKE

PEGGY NOTEBAERT
NATURE MUSEUM ★

W FULLERTON PKWY

CONSERVATORY

LINCOLN
PARK

BELDEN ☆

LINCOLN
PARK ZOO

WEBSTER AVE

5

SOUTH
POND

WISCONSIN ST   FARM IN
THE ZOO

OLD TOWN
TRIANGLE
DISTRICT

W WISCONSIN ST

W WILLOW ST   CRILLY
COURT ★

W EUGENIE ST   FRANKLIN
STATUE

CHICAGO
HISTORY
MUSEUM

W NORTH BLVD   E NORTH
BLVD

SECOND
CITY

ABRAHAM
LINCOLN
MONUMENT ★

NORTH
AVENUE
BEACH
★

547.5 yards
0   250   500 m

OLD TOWN

WRIGLEY FIELD

GRACELAND CEMETERY

ordered by great parks
and beaches – but North
Avenue is the most popular
and *the* place for volleyball
tournaments. Have lunch
on the roof of the sleek,
22,000-square-ft boat-
shaped beach house, with
great views of the lake and
downtown. Just south, Oak
Street Beach is worth a visit too.

**Old Town Triangle
District** (C C6)

*Bounded by N Lincoln Ave,
W North Ave, and N Clark St*
In the mid-1900s, one of
the nation's first neighborhood revitalizations saved
this cove of historic
buildings. Many of the
residents were German
immigrants and later,

working-class families.
Now these are some of the
city's toniest residences.

★ **Boystown** (C B3)

→ *3200–3700 N Halsted St
www.boystownchicago.com*
Officially called
Northalsted, this is the
center of Chicago's lesbian-
gay-bisexual-transgender
community and a hub of
restaurants, clubs, and
nightlife.

★ **Elks Veteran
Memorial** (C C4)

→ *2750 N Lakeview Ave
Tel. (773) 755-4876; Mon-Fri
9am–5pm (plus Sat-Sun
10am–5pm mid-April-mid-
Nov); www.elks.org/memorial*
One of grandest public
buildings in the city, its

decadent, ambitious,
marble-laden rotunda is
stunning with a tinge of
gaudy. If you visit, enter
through the imposing
sculpted-metal front doors,
and slip downstairs for a
glimpse of bizarre
memorabilia of the fraternal
organization that built it.

★ **Wrigley Field** (C A2)

→ *N Clark and W Addison sts*
A baseball purist's dream,
and home of the Chicago
Cubs. Behind its famous
red-and-white sign is a
nexus of joy, legend,
history, and heartbreak
that's stood on this corner
since 1914. The park has a
manual scoreboard, natural
grass, ivy-covered walls,

with residential buildings
over the back wall and the
El train easing by in the
background.

★ **Graceland
Cemetery** (C A1)

→ *4001 N Clark St
Tel. (773) 525-1105; Cemetery:
daily 8am–4.30pm; www.
gracelandcemetery.org*
Architects Daniel Burnham,
Louis Sullivan, Mies van der
Rohe, retail giant Marshall
Field, and boxer Jack
Johnson are just a few of
the many prominent
Chicagoans buried here.
Established in 1860, the
cemetery was beautifully
laid out by landscape
architects H. W. S. Cleveland
and Ossian Simonds.

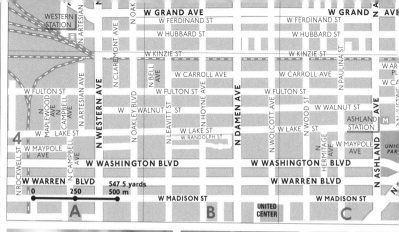

Map area with streets including W GRAND AVE, W FERDINAND ST, W HUBBARD ST, W KINZIE ST, W CARROLL AVE, W FULTON ST, W WALNUT ST, W LAKE ST, W RANDOLPH ST, W WASHINGTON BLVD, W WARREN BLVD, W MADISON ST. WESTERN STATION, ASHLAND STATION, UNITED CENTER.

547.5 yards
0 250 500 m

A   B   C

UKRAINIAN INSTITUTE OF MODERN ART

UKRAINIAN NATIONAL MUSEUM

SIX CORNERS

★ **Wicker Park** (**D** B1)
→ *1425 N Damen Ave*
The triangular park that lends its name to the area is bordered by impressive Victorian mansions, many built after the 1871 fire. Their wealthy, mostly German and Scandinavian owners included a large number of brewing tycoons, earning Hoyne Street the name Beer Baron Row. The area lost much of its luster in the 1960s. Today, however, revitalized and gentrified thanks to the arrival of young professionals, it is a relatively diverse and highly desirable neighborhood.

★ **Division Street** (**D** B-C2)
Over the years, the strip between N Ashland and N Leavitt has been an axis for various ethnic communities and was once nicknamed Polish Broadway. Today it's a thoroughfare for boutique shopping and nighttime barhopping. The street's rich history shows through in locations like the Gold Star Tavern, the Alliance Bakery, the Rainbo Club, once patronized by writer Nelson Algren, and the 1907 terracotta Russian Bathhouse, where you can still enjoy a steam and a massage.

★ **Holy Trinity Russian Orthodox Cathedral** (**D** B2)
→ *1121 N Leavitt St*
Tel. (773) 486-6064
Tours on Sat or by appt
This jewel-like church is tucked away on a residential street. Built thanks to a donation from Tsar Nicholas II, it was designed by Louis Sullivan in 1899 and is considered one of his most inspired small-scale works. Note the intricate woodwork over the front door and the overwhelming beauty of the interior.

★ **Polish Museum of America** (**D** D2)
→ *984 N Milwaukee Ave*
Tel. (773) 384-3352
Fri-Wed 11am–4pm
Three waves of immigration gave Chicago the largest Polish population outside of Warsaw, and this museum has many historical artifacts, fine art, costumes, and a library.

★ **Ukrainian Institute of Modern Art** (**D** A3)
→ *2318 W Chicago Ave*
Tel. (773) 227-5522
Wed, Thu, Sat, Sun noon–4pm; www.uima-chicago.org
Don't dismiss the small UIMA, created in 1971 by combining three storefronts as it contains the world's largest collection of Ukrainian abstract and minimalist works from the 1950s onward. Permanent exhibits include sculptures, paintings, and multimedia works. There's also a varied program of concerts, lectures, and

D

HOLY TRINITY R

DIVISION STREET

WICKER PARK

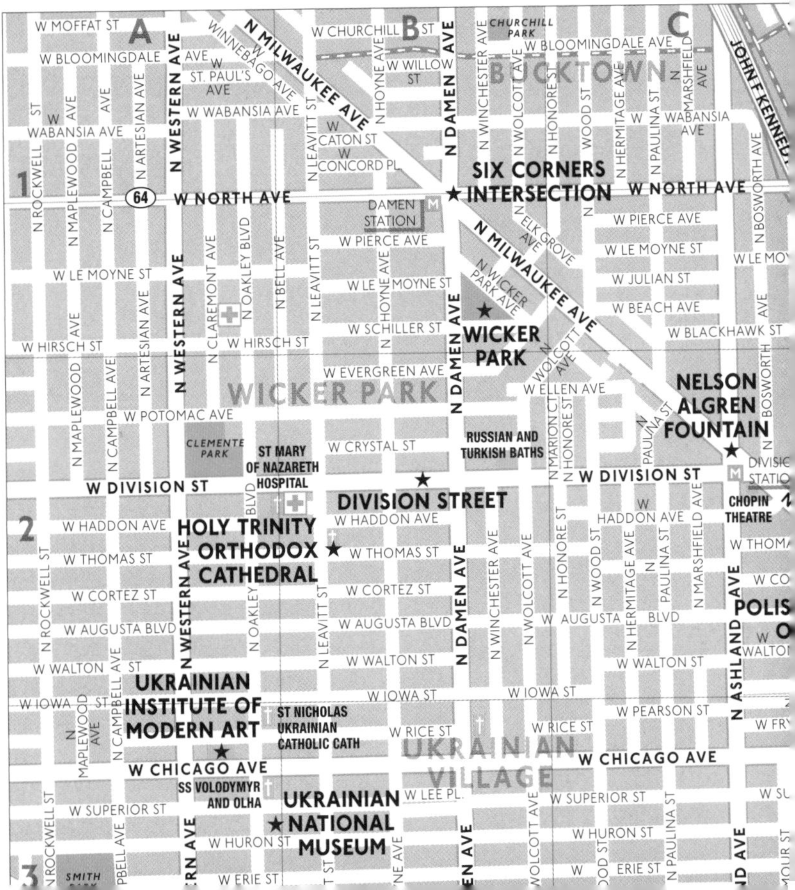

CRUST

SPRING

D

Once home to different immigrant groups – mainly Poles, Mexicans, Ukrainians, and Puerto Ricans – these neighborhoods are made up of graystone and brick buildings and strips of commercial storefronts so typical of Chicago's residential enclaves. A booming art and music scene in Wicker Park has set off a wave of redevelopment that's revitalized the entire area. You can still see the combination of ethnic strongholds of the past mixed with the new in the many restaurants and clubs along Milwaukee Avenue and Division Street. To the southeast, Randolph Street is the area's main culinary drag.

RESTAURANTS

Flo (D D3)
→ 1434 W Chicago Ave (Bishop); Tel. (312) 243-0477 Tue-Fri 8.30am–2.30pm, 6–10pm (11pm Fri); Sat 6–11pm; Sun 9am–2.30pm
The southwestern-style menu at this funky little place offers one of the best brunches in town (avoid Sundays as it will be mobbed). The original breakfast burrito is fantastic, but so are the *huevos rancheros* and chocolate banana pancakes. Great cocktails, too. $8.

Crust (D B2)
→ 2056 W Division St (Hoyne) Tel. (773) 235-5511; Daily 11am–10pm (1am Thu-Sat)
The city's first certified organic restaurant is a hip, modern space with an open kitchen, offering wood-oven flatbread pizza, salads, sandwiches with freshly picked lettuce and vegetables. Try one of Crust's own potent infused vodkas – neat, or in a cocktail. Very pleasant outdoor patio. $12.

Irazu (D A1)
→ 1865 N Milwaukee Ave (Moffat); Tel. (773) 252-5687 Mon-Sat 11.30am–9.30pm
A gem of a family-owned Costa Rican restaurant, popular for its modest prices, laid-back ambience, and delicious food. *Patacones* (fried green plantains), *casado* (a traditional Costa Rican meal), and *gallo pinto* (white rice, black beans, and spices) are all excellent, and the oatmeal shake a must-try. $13.

Mirai (D B2)
→ 2020 W Division St (Damen) Tel. (773) 862-8500 Mon-Sat 5–10pm (11pm Thu-Sat)
This small sushi joint with a minimalist, sleek interior is arguably the best in the city. The fish, prepared by expert chefs, is served by a knowledgeable staff. Lively and young. Reserve to avoid a wait. $15.

West Town Tavern (D D3)
→ 1329 W Chicago Ave (Throop); Tel. (312) 666-6175 Mon-Sat 5–10pm
Tin ceiling, wood floor, and exposed brick walls create the perfect setting for your favorite comfort food: calamari, gnocchi, spring rolls to start and roasted pork, pot roast, or lamb as a main. $18.

Spring (D B1)
→ 2039 W North Ave (Hoyne) Tel. (773) 395-7100; Tue-Sat 5.30–9.30pm (10.30pm Fri-Sat); Sun 5.30–9pm
Enjoy chef Shawn McClain's artful dishes – Maine lobster with crispy rice noodles and a warm

MILWAUKEE AVENUE   RAINBO CLUB   PAPER DOLL

Chinese mustard broth, white miso-potato gnocchi with edamame – in this appealing modern interior, once the Russian Luxor Bathhouse. $30.

Blackbird (D F4)
→ 619 W Randolph St (Desplaines); Tel. (312) 715-0708; Mon-Fri 11.30am-2pm, 6-10.30pm (11.30pm Fri); Sat 5.30-11.30pm
In a sleek, lively, slightly edgy modern setting chef/co-owner Paul Kahen creates such innovative and seasonal American dishes as grilled California sturgeon with stinging nettles. $30. Or try Kahen's equally famous Avec restaurant next door, for Mediterranean-inspired tapas-size dishes cooked in a wood oven.

ICE CREAM, DELI

Margie's Candies (D A1)
→ 1960 N Western Ave (Milwaukee); Daily 9am-midnight (1am Fri-Sat)
Margie's backs up its reputation for cool (the Beatles once hung out here), cozy booths, and ice-cream sundaes that will have you guiltily licking your spoon.

Bari Foods (D D3)
→ 1120 W Grand Ave (May) Tel. (312) 666-0730·

Mon-Sat 8am-6.30pm (6pm Sat); Sun 8am-1pm
Join the daily line at the back of this grocery store for some of the finest submarine sandwiches around. Regular Italian hot or mild is recommended.

BARS, CLUB

Rainbo Club (D B2)
→ 1150 N Damen Ave (Haddon); Tel. (773) 489-5999 Daily 4pm-2am (3am Sat)
This dim bohemian tavern is a neighborhood icon, but since its opening in 1936, the clientele has changed from hardscrabble to hipster.

The Empty Bottle (D A2)
→ 1035 N Western Ave (Cortez); Tel. (773) 276-3600 Mon-Wed 5pm-2am; Thu-Fri 3pm-2am; Sat-Sun noon-3am (2am Sun); www. emptybottle.com
The city's premier venue for independent music, with live acts by up-and-coming bands, local favorites, or veterans of independent music. Cover around $8-10.

Funky Buddha Lounge (D E3)
→ 728 W Grand Ave (Halsted) Tel. (312) 666-1695 Wed-Sun 9pm-2am (3am Sat; midnight Sun)
Weekend nights you'll find

an attractive crowd lined up waiting to get into this dance club with a Middle Eastern-inspired decor. DJs spin house, funk, hip-hop, and are always excellent.

SHOPPING

Alcala's Western Wear (D C3)
→ 1733 W Chicago Ave (Hermitage) Tel. (312) 226-0152; Thu-Fri Mon 9.30am-7pm (8pm Thu); Sun 9.30am-5pm
Great selection of hats, belt buckles, embroidered shirts, and boots by Tony Lama, Lucchese, Justin in all kind of skins.

Roslyn (D off C1)
→ 2035 N Damen Ave (Armitage) Tel. (773) 489-1511; Tue-Sat 11am-7pm; Sun noon-6pm
A homey shop that stocks only four of each style, making every purchase virtually unique.

City Soles / Niche (D B1)
→ 1566 N Damen Ave (North); Tel. (773) 489-2001 Mon-Sat 10am-7pm (8pm Thu-Sat); Sun 11am-6pm
A high-end yet funky shoe store also selling jewelry and handbags. Broad selection and great flair.

Paper Doll (D B2)
→ 2048 W Division St (Damen); Tel. (773) 227-6950

Daily 11am-7pm (5pm Sat-Sun)
This stationery and gift shop has unique greeting cards and local letterpress cards and also hip shirts, candles, magnets, picture frames, and more.

Milwaukee Ave (D B1-C2)
→ N Ashland to N Damen aves
One of the best shopping spots in the city. You'll find American Apparel, Urban Outfitters – but also a lot of great boutiques selling jewelry, clothes, shoes, records, etc.

Hejfina (D B1)
→ 1529 N Milwaukee Ave (North); Tel. (773) 772-0002 Tue-Sat 11am-7pm; Sun noon-6pm
The modern aesthetics of Alexander Wang and Helmut Lang fit in perfectly. Installations by emerging Chicago artists complement shoes, clothes, and accessories that are avant- garde and functional.

Bess & Loie (D E4)
→ 1015 W Lake St (Morgan) Tel. (312) 226-2247 Mon-Sat noon (11am Thu-Sat)-7pm; Sun noon-5pm
Great bags by boutique designers Bocue and Helena de Natalio and baubles by Chicagoan Michelle Rubin.

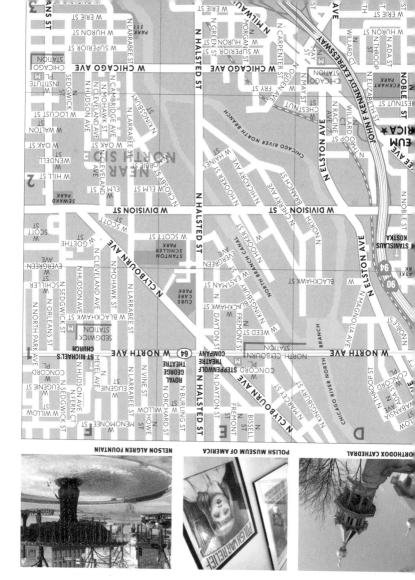

NELSON ALGREN FOUNTAIN

POLISH MUSEUM OF AMERICA

ORTHODOX CATHEDRAL

HARPO STUDIOS

RANDOLPH STREET

...nporary exhibitions.

**Nelson Algren
...untain (D** C2)
...W Division St (N Ashland)
...lson Algren once said his
...ection for Chicago's
...rsh, scrappy beauty was
...e loving a woman with a
...oken nose. You may well
...d lovelier lovelies. But
...ver a lovely so real'. This
...ot is decades removed
...m Algren's hardscrabble
...ventures on Division
...reet, but if you spend a
...w moments on the small
...angular island, you can
...ll see what Algren meant.

**Ukrainian National
...useum (D** A3)
*2249 W Superior St
(312) 421-8020; Thu-Sun*

11am–4pm; Mon-Wed by appt
This 160-acre area was once
home to more than 25,000
people of Ukrainian descent
and is still the site of many
of their institutions and
restaurants, including this
fascinating museum of
Ukrainian history, opened
in 1952, that exhibits
costumes, ceramics, and
pysanky, Ukraine's beautifully decorated Easter eggs.

**★ Six Corners
intersection (D** B1)
*→ W Milwaukee / N Damen /
W North*
In the 1990s artists started
moving into Wicker Park,
transforming it from rough
to hip. The area now leads
a double life, still buzzing

with the trendy art crowd
but increasingly dominated
by an affluent professional
one, which followed a few
years later. Coffeehouses,
boutiques and salons,
upscale lounges, flashy
dance clubs, rock-and-roll
spots, and restaurants
radiate from this
intersection, where North
Avenue divides Wicker Park
from Bucktown to the north.
Probably the best nightlife
in town.

★ Harpo Studios (D E4)
*→ 1058 W Washington Blvd
Tel. (312) 591-9222*
Flip the name around and
you get 'Oprah'. This is
where Chicago's media
queen shoots her show.

Tours of the pink complex
are not available, though
it's worth a look if you're in
the neighborhood. You can,
however, attend a taping,
but competition for tickets
is fierce so plan ahead:
call early and often.

★ Randolph Street (D E4)
*→ S Jefferson St and
N Ogden Ave*
Some of the city's best
restaurants and a number
of overpriced and slinky
bars grace this strip,
occasionally referred to
as 'Restaurant Row'.
Avec (no. 615), Blackbird
(no. 619), Sushi Wabi
(no. 842), One Sixty Blue
(no. 1400) are just a few
recommended addresses.

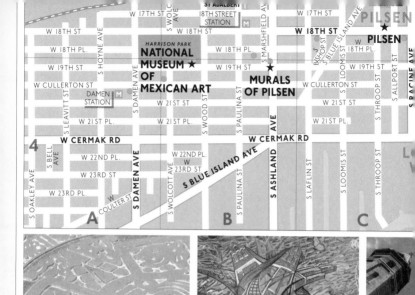

PILSEN

PILSEN MURALS

OLD ST PATRICK

★ Greektown (E D1)
In the 1840s Greek immigrants streamed into Chicago, many settling just west of downtown to be close to the wholesale food warehouses, where they worked. By the 1930s there were 30,000 first- and second-generation Greek Americans. It's not the hub of Greek population it once was – but it is full of many authentic tavernas on S Halsted, between Monroe and Van Buren.

★ Little Italy (E C2)
→ *Between S Morgan St and S Ashland Ave*
Chicago's Little Italy is smaller than it used to be, but it is a flourishing area,

thanks to a large influx of young people. Taylor Street is the hub of the neighborhood and has a great variety of restaurants, grocery stores, and shops. Look out for a few rough spots near outgoing housing projects (between Racine and Loomis).

★ National Museum of Mexican Art (E B4)
→ *1852 W 19th St*
Tel. (312) 738-1503
Tue-Sun 10am–5pm
Just off Pilsen's main thoroughfare is the first museum in the region devoted to Mexican art and the largest Latino museum in the United States. Founded in 1982 by two

teachers, the museum houses a collection of artwork from Mexico and the US. The Day of the Dead Festival (Nov 1) organized by the museum is the largest in the nation.

★ Jane Addams' Hull-House Museum (E D2)
→ *800 S Halsted St*
Tel. (312) 413-5353; Tue-Fri 10am–4pm; Sun noon–4pm
In 1889 pioneering social workers Addams and Ellen G. Starr founded this innovative settlement house, to help the urban poor. Only 2 of the original 13 buildings remain, which now house the museum. In 1931 Addams became the first American woman

to win the Nobel Peace Prize. Today the organization, with headquarters in the Loop, is still going strong.

★ Union Station (E E1)
→ *210 S Canal St*
Daily 5.30am–midnight
In the 1950s and 1960s, Chicago was the rail cente of the nation, with more than 100,000 travelers passing through daily. Th grand station has a waitin room with arching skyligh and marble staircases – featured in Brian DePalm movie *The Untouchables* – and is well worth seeing.

★ Pilsen (E C3)
→ *18th St (Racine and Woo*
In the 1870s Bohemian

E

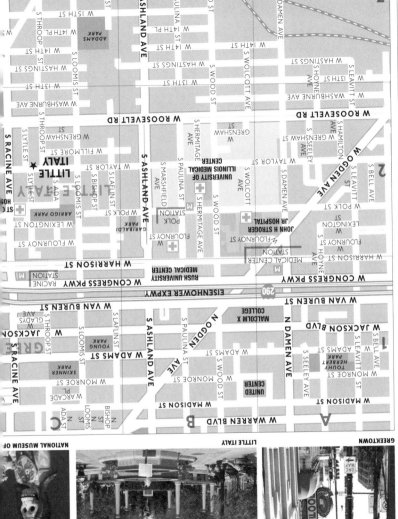

GREEKTOWN

LITTLE ITALY

NATIONAL MUSEUM OF

On the Near South and Southwest sides are four of the city's enduring ethnic pockets. Just west of downtown, Greektown wraps around Halsted Street. Below, Little Italy along Taylor Street took some hits from surrounding development, but mainstays like Mario's Italian Lemonade protect the neighborhood's identity. Pilsen is the hub of Chicago's Mexican community, the second largest in the nation, though an arty hipster element has also moved in. East of Pilsen, along Wentworth and Archer avenues, Chicago's Chinatown is a lively, bustling area full of shops and restaurants.

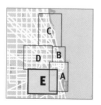

NUEVO LEON

FEIDA BAKERY

RESTAURANTS

Al #1 Italian Beef (E D2)
→ *1079 W Taylor St (Carpenter)*
Tel. (312) 226-4017; Mon-Sat 9am (10am Sat)–midnight
A local institution, whose specialty is the beef sandwich: bread loaded with thinly sliced Italian beef, peppers, and spices – delicious. $5–8.

Lawrence Fisheries (E E4)
→ *2120 S Canal St (Cermak)*
Tel. (312) 225-2113
Daily, 24 hours
A family-run business since 1950, with a dining room that looks onto the river and skyline. It specializes in fried shrimp and fish 'chips', as well as oysters, cod, clams, scallops, and frogs' legs – sold by the pound. Takeout available. $7.

Joy Yee Noodle Shop (E F4)
→ *2139 S China Place (Princeton)*
Tel. (312) 328-0001
Daily 11am–10.30pm
The Chinatown outpost of a mini-empire, it serves classic pan-Asian cuisine popular with the younger crowd for its low prices and big portions – lemongrass shrimp, coconut Thai curry seafood, or

Japanese tofu with two mushrooms. A serious drinks list: shaved ice, fruit and tapioca freezes, tapioca milk tea, etc. $9.

Nuevo Leon (E C3)
→ *1515 W 18th St (Laflin)*
Tel. (312) 421-1517
Daily 7am–11.30pm
The Gutierrez family has been operating this brightly painted Pilsen favorite since the early 1960s. Try the enchiladas (corn tortillas dipped in sauce) or fajitas *norteñas* (skirt steak with green peppers, onions, and guacamole), two of the house's popular dishes. BYOB. $10.

Phoenix (E F4)
→ *2131 S Archer Ave (Cermak)*
Tel. (312) 328-0848
Daily 9am (8am Sat-Sun)– 3pm, 5–9.30pm (10.30pm Fri-Sat); dim sum until 3pm
On weekends, people pack into the huge dining room for the carts of varied dim sum, regarded by many as the best in town; it also has a long menu of classic Mandarin dishes. $12.

Santorini (E D1)
→ *138 S Halsted St (Monroe)*
Tel. (312) 829-8820; Daily 11am–midnight (1am Fri-Sat)
A cozy white stucco room with wood chairs, copper pots hanging from the beams, plates on the walls, and a fireplace for those

MANNY'S (partially cut off as "ANNY'S")

MARIO'S ITALIAN LEMONADE

ATHENIAN CANDLE

cold Chicago winter nights. Fresh seafood is flown in daily and cooked with olive oil imported from the family farm in Sparta. $15.

Athena (E D1)

→ 212 S Halsted St (Adams)
Tel. (312) 655-0000; Daily 11am–midnight (1am Fri-Sat)
What gives Athena a leg up on its neighbors is the outdoor patio with a view of downtown, for eating outside when the weather is right. Good traditional Greek cuisine. Mains $15.

Rosebud (E C2)

→ 1500 W Taylor St (Laflin)
Tel. (312) 942-1117; Mon-Sat noon–10.30pm (11.30pm Fri-Sat); Sun noon–10pm
Classic Italian dishes prepared well, without too many liberties, and portions to tame big appetites. $19. If Rosebud's too busy, try RoSal's down the road, at no. 1154 (312-243-2357).

CAFÉ, BAKERIES, ICE-CREAM PARLOR

Sweet Maple Cafe (E C2)

→ 1339 W Taylor St (Ada)
Tel. (312) 243-8908
Daily 7am–2pm
This Southern-style breakfast joint is very comforting. The basics of biscuits, gravy, and grits

are excellent, but it's the specialties like seasonal fruit pancakes that make it truly fabulous.

Manny's (E E2)

→ 1141 S Jefferson St (Grenshaw)
Mon-Sat 5am–8pm
A beloved, casual coffee shop-deli worth a visit if you're in the area. Try the potato pancakes, stacked pastrami sandwich, or meatloaf – all delicious.

Nuevo Leon Bakery (E B3)

→ 1634 W 18th St (Marshfield)
Tel. (312) 243-5977; Daily 5.30am (6am Sat-Sun)–9pm
Not connected to the restaurant, but it is just down the street; get a coffee and try the Mexican wedding cookies, the empanadas, or corn gorditas.

Feida Bakery (E F4)

→ 2228 S Wentworth Ave (Cermak); Tel. (312) 808-1113
Daily 7am–9pm
The best bakery in Chinatown: go for the cha siu bao (barbecued pork bun), moon cake, or don tot (custard tart).

Mario's Italian Lemonade (E D2)

→ 1068 W Taylor St (Carpenter); Daily 11am–midnight (May-Sep); closes earlier if cold and slow

On hot nights, Chicagoans mob the sidewalk, lining up at Mario's wooden stand. The stellar fresh Italian ices are made from chilled lemonade, fresh fruit, and syrups in many flavors. Cantaloupe and peach must be tried.

BARS

Drum & Monkey (E C2)

→ 1435 W Taylor St (Loomis)
Tel. (312) 563-1874
Mon-Thu 3pm–2am;
Fri-Sun 11am–2am
A cozy pub named after a popular Glasgow drinking hole, with a 1940s tin ceiling, Tiffany-inspired lighting, jukebox, and pool table. Imported pints on tap, and decent takes on fish and chips and shepherd's pie.

Skylark (E D4)

→ 2149 S Halsted St (Cermak); Tel. (312) 948-5275
Daily 4pm–2am (3am Sat)
An endearingly dank cave of a bar, and a haven for those Pilsen hipsters. Sit in one of the booths and listen to jazz on Mondays, try the Simpsons pinball machine or see if the photo booth is working. Cheap beer, and surprisingly good food – burgers, BBQ pork sandwich, Tater Tots.

SHOPPING

Mestiza (E D3)

→ 1010 W 18th St (Miller)
Tel. (312) 563-0132
Tue-Sun 11.30am–7pm (4.30pm Sun)
This neighborhood shop is packed with charm, Latin culture, jewelry, pottery clothes, and crafts made by Chicago artists.

New Maxwell Street Market (E E2)

→ W Roosevelt Rd and S Canal St; Sun 7am–3pm
After 120 years, the original open-air market was closed and relocated here. Weather permitting, some 400 vendors set up every week to sell tools, clothes, household goods, fresh produce, jewelry, and electronics. Live blues music, and excellent Mexican food stands.

Athenian Candle (E D1)

→ 300 S Halsted St (Jackson)
Tel. (312) 332-6988
Mon-Tue, Thu-Sat 9.30am–6pm
Having catered to the West Side's Greek Orthodox community for almost a century, this store is packed with candles, 'evil eye' stones, and concoctions that promise luck, protection, and success.

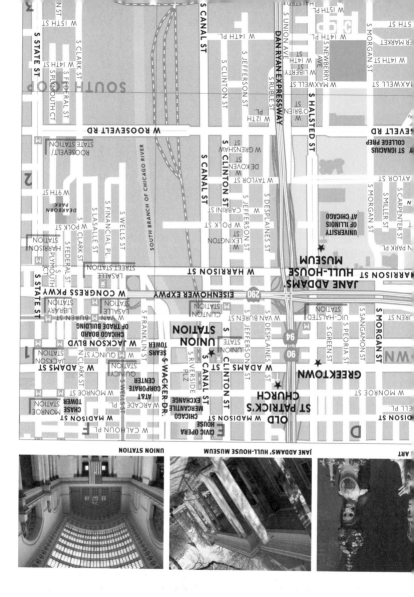

UNION STATION

JANE ADDAMS, HULL-HOUSE MUSEUM

ART

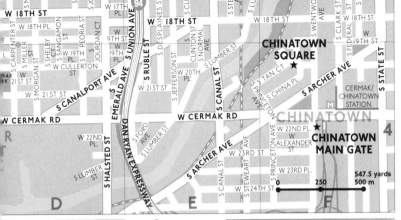

CHINATOWN MAIN GATE

CHINATOWN SQUARE

immigrants settled in an area they named after one [of] their homeland's largest [ci]ties. By the 1960s, [h]owever, a large working-[cl]ass Mexican community [h]ad arrived, pushed south [by] the building of the [un]iversity. Lively and [c]olorful, it is currently [ge]tting gentried, and is [b]ecoming one of the city's [tr]endier areas, with the [ar]rival of many artists; it is [al]so one the best places in [th]e city for Mexican food.

[M]urals of Pilsen
[B]uilding on the tradition [of] Mexican painters like [D]iego Rivera and José [O]rozco, a group of Pilsen [ar]tists has graced the

neighborhood with a spectrum of beautiful, large-scale public paintings and mosaics. East to west, here are the highlights, which provide a great walking tour.
→ *1900 S Carpenter St (Bill Campillo)*
→ *1831 S Racine Ave (Raymond Patlán)*
→ *S Bishop and E 18th sts (collaborative mural on the Taller Mestizarte building)*
→ *1919 S Ashland Ave (Jeff Zimmerman)*
→ *1645 W 18th Pl. (Francisco Mendoza and students)*
→ *1900 W Cullerton St (Hector Duarte)*
→ *2000 S Damen Ave (Juan Chavez)*

→ *2009 S Western Ave (Hector Duarte – off map)*
★ **Old St Patrick's Church (E** E1)
→ *700 W Adams St*
Tel. *(312) 648-1021*
This church, which survived the 1871 fire, claims to be the oldest public building in town. Built in 1852–6, its stained-glass windows depict Irish saints, scholars, and missionaries.
★ **Chinatown Main Gate (E** F4)
→ *W Cermak Rd (S Wentworth)*
Though smaller than its counterparts in other American cities, this is a picturesque spot. When you're here, wander

Cermak, Wentworth and Archer – but don't go too far east of the CTA train station as the area gets a bit dicey.
★ **Chinatown Square (E** F4)
→ *S China Pl.*
Built in the 1990s, this landmark is defined by statues that represent all animals of the Chinese zodiac and anchors the newer commercial area of Chinatown. It doesn't look as historic as Wentworth Avenue, but the pedestrian mall around it is home to some of the area's best restaurants and often has better prices than the southern main drag.

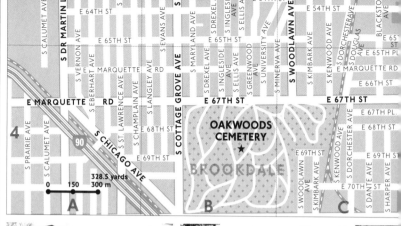

ROBIE HOUSE

PROMONTORY POINT

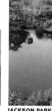

JACKSON PARK

★ DuSable Museum of African American History (**F** B2)

→ *740 E 56th Pl.*
Tel. (773) 947-0600; Tue-Sat 10am–5pm; Sun noon–5pm
The oldest museum of its kind in the US, it's devoted to the history, art, and culture of African Americans. The collections include art, personal affects of historical figures like scholar W. E. B. Du Bois and poet Langston Hughes, as well as artifacts from the 19th and 20th centuries, and the slave era.

Fountain of Time (**F** B3)

→ *5900 S Cottage Grove Ave*
Built in 1922 by Lorado Taft, it was supposed to have a counterpart at the other end of the Midway, but the 'Fountain of Creation' was never designed. Peek around the back for a man with a mustache – a self-portrait of Taft.

★ University of Chicago (**F** B2)

→ *E 55th to E 61st sts, between Cottage Grove and Woodlawn*
This showcase of classic architectural beauty is the central pillar of Hyde Park's intellectually and politically active community, which holds a powerful and historic niche in the city's power structure. Founded with money from oil baron John D. Rockefeller, the university is speckled with museums and hosts many public events. Mike Nichols, Susan Sontag, and Philip Glass are among its former graduates. Highlights of the U of C include: the **Oriental Institute**, *1155 E 58th St*, a museum of the ancient Near East; the **Smart Museum**, *550 S Greenwood Ave*, the university's main art museum; and **Bond Chapel**, *1050 E 59th St*, an architectural gem (1926) with delicate wood carvings and stained glass by Charles Connick.

Rockefeller Memorial Chapel (**F** C2)

→ *5850 S Woodlawn Ave*
Tel. (773) 702-2100
Daily 8am–4pm

This limestone giant was designed by Bertram Grosvenor Goodhue, completed in 1928, and named for benefactors Joh D. Rockefeller Sr and Jr. It i a striking modern riff on Gothic, and a great stop o the Midway.

The Renaissance Society (**F** B2)

→ *5811 S Ellis Ave, Bergman Gallery, Cobb Hall 418*
Tel. (773) 702-8670; Tue-Sun 10am (noon Sat-Sun)–5pm
www.renaissancesociety.org
This long-standing treasur of an art gallery puts on fiv remarkable contemporary art exhibitions every year and has a schedule of edg intelligent lectures and

F

Map Labels

UNIVERSITY OF CHICAGO

ROBIE HOUSE

SMART MUSEUM OF ART

RENAISSANCE SOCIETY

ORIENTAL INSTITUTE

BOND CHAPEL

ROCKEFELLER MEMORIAL CHAPEL

INTERNATIONAL HOUSE

FOUNTAIN OF TIME

DUSABLE MUSEUM OF AFRICAN AMERICAN HISTORY

AMERICAN MUSEUM OF AFRICAN HISTORY

WASHINGTON PARK

HYDE PARK

MIDWAY PLAISANCE PARK

MIDWAY STUDIOS

LAGOON

GENERAL JONES ARMORY

CHICAGO OSTEOPATHIC HOSPITAL

HELLER HOUSE

K.A.M. ISAIAH ISRAEL TEMPLE

PROVIDENT HOSPITAL OF COOK COUNTY

DREXEL SQUARE PARK

CHRISTOPHER B BOUTON HOUSE

WARREN MC ARTHUR HOUSE

BLOSSOM HOUSE

KENWOOD HOUSE

MADISON PARK

KENWOOD COMM. PARK

ELM PLAYLOT PARK "278"

STOUT PARK

WILLOW PARK

NICHOLS PARK

SPRUCE PARK

Streets

S. LAKE PARK AVE, S. HARPER AVE, S. BLACKSTONE AVE, S. DORCHESTER AVE, S. KENWOOD AVE, S. KIMBARK AVE, S. WOODLAWN AVE, S. UNIVERSITY AVE, S. GREENWOOD AVE, S. ELLIS AVE, S. INGLESIDE AVE, S. DREXEL AVE, S. DREXEL BLVD, S. COTTAGE GROVE AVENUE, S. MARYLAND AVE, S. RIDGEWOOD AVE, S. RHODES AVE, S. CHAMPLAIN AVE, S. LANGLEY AVE, S. EVANS AVE, S. VINCENNES AVE, S. ST. LAWRENCE AVE, S. FORRESTVILLE AVE, S. DR MARTIN LUTHER KING JR DR, S. CALUMET AVE, S. PRAIRIE AVE, S. EBERHART AVE, S. VERNON AVE, S. RUSSEL DR, S. DR MARTIN LUTHER KING JR. DR., MORGAN DR., RAINEY DR., PAYNE DR., ELSWORTH DR., BEST DR., PLAISANCE DR., COTTAGE GROVE AVE.

E 48TH ST, E 49TH ST, E 50TH ST, E 51ST ST, E 53RD ST, E 54TH ST, E 55TH ST, E 56TH ST, E 57TH STREET, E 58TH ST, E 59TH ST, E 60TH ST, E 61ST ST, E 62ND ST

E HYDE PARK BLVD, E GARFIELD BLVD, E 55TH PL GARFIELD BLVD, KING JR DR.

Stations: 51ST STREET STATION, 55TH PL. GARFIELD STATION, 56TH ST STATION, 57TH STREET STATION, 59TH ST STATION, HYDE PARK HIST. SOC. STATION, ROSAL VILLAS

Photo Captions

DUSABLE MUSEUM OF AFRICAN AMERICAN HISTORY

FOUNTAIN OF TIME

UNIVERSITY OF CHICAGO

A short jaunt from downtown is the affluent Kenwood neighborhood, where you will pass historic homes designed by Frank Lloyd Wright – the George W. Blossom, Warren McArthur, and Isidore Heller houses – and Prairie School mansions. Six blocks south, Hyde Park is one of Chicago's more integrated neighborhoods. It revolves around the University of Chicago and is an intellectual, social and political nexus. The nearby Jackson Park, site of the 1893 World's Columbian Exposition, occupies most of the eastern part of the Woodlawn area. Attractions are numerous, but note that there are some dicey areas close by, particularly west and southwest of U of C.

LEM'S

MEDICI ON 57TH

RESTAURANTS

Valois (F C1)
→ 1518 E 53rd St (Harper)
Tel. (773) 667-0647
Daily 6am–10pm
Comfort comes in big portions at this neighborhood cafeteria dating to 1921. You'll understand the motto 'See Your Food' as soon as you grab a tray and browse the all-day breakfasts, short ribs, T-bone steaks, and chicken potpies. No alcohol. $8.

Lem's (off map **F**, south of A4)
→ 311 E 75th St (Prairie)
Tel. (773) 994-2428
Daily 2pm–2am
(4am Fri-Sat)
This legendary local barbecue spot has been smoking ribs since the 1950s, when the Lemon brothers moved here from Mississippi. No dining room, so plan to walk out with a bag full of tender pork ribs layered on fries and white bread, smothered in tangy sauce and spicy hotlinks. $8.

Medici on 57th (F C2)
→ 1327 E 57th St (Kenwood)
Tel. (773) 667-7394
Mon-Fri 11am–11pm;
Sat-Sun 7am–midnight
(11pm Sun)
This local favorite with exposed-brick walls, cozy booths, and a beautiful rooftop patio has a beloved menu of pizzas, burgers, and sandwiches (the grilled tuna steak with ginger-sesame mayonnaise is worth trying). Keep some room for a fudge-banana-nut milkshake. BYOB. $9. Next door, the Medici Bakery is one of the best in the city. The fruit tarts, croissants, bread, and muffins are all excellent.

Uncle John's (F A4)
→ 337 E 69th St (Calumet)
Tel. (773) 892-1233
Mon-Sat 11am–10pm
(12.45am Fri-Sat)
Properly slow-smoked ribs make this BBQ spot celebrated among connoisseurs. Three pieces of advice: call first to make sure the ribs are ready, don't order hotlinks if you don't like real spice, and, last but not least, don't miss this one if you like barbecue. $9.

Army & Lou's (off map **F**, south of A4)
→ 422 E 75th St (Vernon)
Tel. (773) 483-3100
Wed-Mon 9am–10pm
After more than 60 years in business, this place is a city institution, where local politicians come to eat Southern comfort

ODLAWN TAP   NEW CHECKERBOARD LOUNGE   SEMINARY CO-OP BOOKSTORE

food. Don't miss the sweet potato pie. $10.

Dixie Kitchen and Bait Shop (F C1)
→ 5225 S Harper Ave (52nd) Harper Court Shopping Center; Tel. (773) 363-4943 Daily 11am–10pm (11pm Fri-Sat)
With light shades made of old bait buckets and popcorn tins, and fishing tackle, jugs, old beer and soda bottles as decoration, you could be on a Southern back porch. Self-described as 'pan-Southern,' Dixie Kitchen has everything from North Carolina pulled pork and fried green tomatoes to crawfish étouffée and gumbo. $12.

Rajun Cajun (F C1)
→ 1459 E 53rd St (Blackstone) Tel. (773) 955-1145 Mon-Sat 11am–9.30pm; Sun noon–9pm
This combination Indian/soul food restaurant has excellent curries (spicy vegetable, lamb, fish, etc.) with sides of samosas and basmati rice, and fried or tandoori chicken. If you don't mind things on the spicier side, you may find yourself among the loyal local following. $10.

La Petite Folie (F C2)
→ 1504 E 55th St (Harper) Tel. (773) 493-1394 Tue-Fri 11.30am–2pm, 5pm–last reservation at 8pm; Sat-Sun 5pm–last reservation at 8pm
This is the area's fine-dining option. The vibe is unpretentious, and the prices are reasonable, and the food traditional French: salade niçoise, smoked pheasant salad, sautéed snails with parsley, and medallions of venison are a few of the dishes on offer. $22. The $35 pretheater menu (5–6.30pm) is an excellent value for the money.

CAFÉ, BARS, MUSIC

Istria Café (F C2)
→ 1520 E 57th St (Lake Park) Tel. (773) 955-2556 Daily 6.30am (7am Sat; 7.30am Sun)–7.30pm
Family-owned and -operated café with a unique flair tucked under train tracks. Good coffee, pastry, panini, and freshly made gelato. A great pit stop for Museum of Science and Industry and Jackson Park visitors.

Woodlawn Tap (F C2)
→ 1172 E 55th St (Woodlawn) Tel. (773) 643-5516

Mon-Fri 10.30am–2am; Sat-Sun 11am–3am (2am Sun)
A beloved hangout for students and locals since 1948, known as Jimmy's after its late owner, Jimmy Wilson. A no-frills joint, good for catching a game on the TV, or having a beer in one of the back rooms. Basic, but good, bar food. Often live jazz and blues on Sunday.

New Apartment Lounge
(off map F, south of A4)
→ 504 E 75th St (Eberhart) Tel. (773) 483-7728 Mon-Fri 3.30pm–4am; Sat-Sun 3pm–5am (4am Sun)
This Christmas-light-laced neighborhood bar is a cozy spot for a drink. Chicago jazz saxophone legend Von Freeman plays here every Tuesday night. For daily music, head one block west, to Lee's Unleaded Blues (7401 S Chicago Ave), one of the South Side's better-known blues bars.

New Checkerboard Lounge (F C1)
→ 5201 S Harper Ave (52nd) Tel. (773) 684-1472 Daily 11am–2am www.checkerjazz.org
This other famous South Side club known for jazz and blues closed a few years ago and was reborn in this location. The crowd

is a mix of U of C students and Hyde Park locals. Expect a cover that varies to match the act onstage.

SHOPPING

57th Street Books (F C2)
→ 1301 E 57th St (Kimbark) Tel. (773) 684-1300; Daily 10am–9pm (8pm Sat-Sun)
Near U of C, your main shopping option is books. This lovely ground-level shop has a cozy reading room in the back.

Seminary Co-op Bookstore (F B2)
→ 5757 S University Ave (58th); Tel. (773) 752-4381 Mon-Fri 8.30am–9pm; Sat 10am–6pm; Sun 9am–6pm
A sight to behold, this bookstore has over 100,000 titles. The 'front table' is considered a place of honor by U of C academics.

Hyde Park Records (F C1)
→ 1377 E 53rd St (Dorchester) Tel. (773) 288-6588 Daily 11am–8pm
Because the intellectual Hyde Park factions cannot live on books alone, they go to this independent storefront music shop to buy CDs and records.

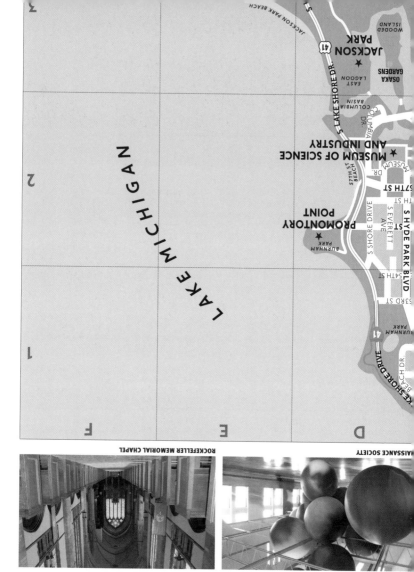

ROCKEFELLER MEMORIAL CHAPEL

...NAISSANCE SOCIETY

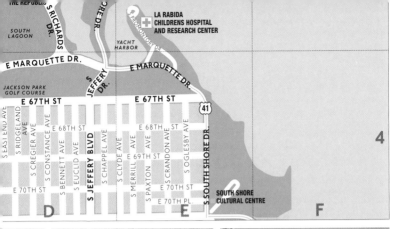

THE REPUBLIC

SOUTH LAGOON

S RICHARDS DR.

LA RABIDA CHILDRENS HOSPITAL AND RESEARCH CENTER

YACHT HARBOR

E MARQUETTE DR.

E MARQUETTE DR.

JACKSON PARK GOLF COURSE

S JEFFERY DR.

E 67TH ST

E 67TH ST

41

S EAST END AVE
S RIDGELAND AVE
S CREGIER AVE
S CONSTANCE AVE
S BENNETT AVE
S EUCLID AVE
S JEFFERY BLVD
S CHAPPEL AVE
S CLYDE AVE
S MERRILL AVE
S PAXTON AVE
S CRANDON AVE
S OGLESBY AVE
S SOUTH SHORE DR.

E 68TH ST
E 68TH ST
E 69TH ST
E 70TH ST
E 70TH ST
E 70TH PL.

SOUTH SHORE CULTURAL CENTRE

D   E   F   4

GARDEN

MUSEUM OF SCIENCE AND INDUSTRY

OAKWOODS CEMETERY

ates tackling challenging ics other galleries might too timid to wrestle with.

Robie House (F C2)
→757 S Woodlawn Ave
(708) 848-1976; Daily
m–3pm (3.30pm Sat-Sun)
epitome of the Prairie
ool style, it was
igned by Frank Lloyd
ght in 1908–09 for
ycle and motorcycle heir
derick C. Robie and has
eresting rectangular
nes and a bold
ymmetry.

Promontory Point (F D2)
5491 South Shore Dr.
ly 7am–9pm
s isolated treasure of a
k can be reached by a
efront bike path or

through a tunnel on 55th Street. 'The Point' is deeply loved by Chicagoans for its limestone blocks along the shore and for its panoramic views of the lake.

★ **Oakwoods Cemetery (F** B-C4)
→ 1035 E 67th St
Mon-Fri 8am-4.15pm;
Sat-Sun 8.30am–dusk
The curving paths of Chicago's oldest private cemetery lead you in circles through the city's history. There are places of national significance, like the Confederate Mound Memorial – the largest monument to Southern soldiers in the North marks the grave of more than

6,000 prisoners of war. Chicago's first black mayor, Harold Washington, Olympic great Jesse Owens, and former mayor William 'Big Bill' Thompson are among the many prominent figures resting here.

★ **Jackson Park (F** D2-3)
→ 6401 S Stony Island Ave
Tel. (773) 256-0903
Frederick Law Olmsted designed most of the park's 650 acres in time for it to receive the World's Columbian Exposition in 1893. Don't miss Daniel Chester French's *Republic*, a 24-ft-high golden replica of his original 65-ft work erected for the Exposition, and the serene Japanese

Osaka Garden on the lagoon's Wooded Island.
Museum of Science and Industry (F D2)
→ 57th St and Lake Shore Dr.
Tel. (773) 684-1414
Daily 9.30am (11am Sun)–
4pm; www.msichicago.org
This huge neoclassical structure is the last remaining building of the Columbian Exposition and houses one of Chicago's most popular attractions with 14 acres of exhibits and hands-on, interactive displays. Highlights include a U-505 submarine, two flight simulators, a working replica of a coal mine, a chick hatchery, and a walk-through human heart.

DRIVING

Chicago's metropolitan area is one of the most congested in the country, so driving isn't recommended, nor is it necessary as the public transportation system is accessible.

Speed limits
30mph on city streets; 55mph on the expressway (45mph in parts of downtown).

Parking
Time-consuming and expensive downtown and close to downtown. If using parking meters, bring plenty of quarters because it's the only coin accepted. Wherever you park, though, read all posted signs, as the city is famous for posting many, sometimes conflicting, signs, and city police love to give tickets.

Fees
→ Parking meters : $10–18 / four hours
→ Downtown garages: $20–40 overnight
→ Valet parking: $10–20 plus tip

TAXIS

Easy to catch downtown and in the areas north and northwest of downtown. Harder to find farther from downtown, though you can call to get picked up. A lit numbered sign on the cab means it is available.
→ Yellow Cab Tel. (312) 829-4222
→ Flash Cab Chicago Tel. (773) 561-4444

UNION STATION

THE EL

THE EL

Division subway stop is one block away. From $129.
Majestic Hotel (C B2)
→ 528 W Brompton Ave (Lake Shore); Tel. (773) 404-3499 www.cityinns.com
On a residential street near Wrigley Field, you might not expect the cozy vibe you'll get here. English country estate decor and friendly staff. $139–259, incl. breakfast.

Carleton of Oak Park Hotel & Motor Inn
→ 1110 Pleasant St, Oak Park Tel. (708) 848-5000 www.carltonhotel.com
A great place to stay in Oak Park, this small 70-year-old hotel has only 25 rooms, done in American colonial style. The train into the city is just down the street. $148–198.

Hotel Blake (A B3)
→ 500 S Dearborn St (Congress)
Tel. (312) 986-1234 www.hotelblake.com

In the former headquarters for the Morton Salt Company, this hotel has 162 smart rooms in earth-toned colors; a day spa; and a renowned restaurant, Custom House (see **A**). $169–279.

Willows Hotel (C B4)
→ 555 W Surf St (Broadway)
Tel. (773) 528-8400 www.cityinns.com/willows
This 55-room hotel is in a residential area, two blocks from the lake. Freshly made afternoon cookies, complimentary breakfast, and a helpful staff. Very good value for money. $167–339.

Hilton Chicago (A B3)
→ 720 S Michigan Ave (Balbo); Tel. (312) 922-4400 www.hilton.com
This South Michigan giant – it has 1,544 rooms and suites – faces the lake and the south end of Grant Park. It's almost as massive as its ballroom (where

Harrison Ford shot the final scene of The Fugitive) is decadent. $179–289.

Comfort Inn & Suites Downtown (B B5)
→ 15 E Ohio St (State)
Tel. (312) 894-0900 www.chicagocomfortinn.com
Budget friendly with 130 rooms and a great location. Despite a clumsy combination of aesthetic styles, it beats your average budget chain. $189–289.

Ambassador East (B B2)
→ 1301 N State Pkwy (Goethe)
Tel. (312) 787-7200; www.the ambassadoreasthotel.com
A Chicago classic, this hotel is known for hosting celebrities – as is the historic Pump Room restaurant downstairs. $189–339.

$200–$320

Hotel Burnham (A B2)
→ 1 W Washington St (State)
Tel. (312) 782-1111

AIRPORTS

www.flychicago.com

O'Hare International
→ 17 miles northwest of downtown
For international and domestic flights.

Midway International
→ 10 miles southwest of downtown

To the city center
By El train
→ From O'Hare: with the Blue Line; 45 mins; $2
→ From Midway, with the Orange Line; 35 mins; $2
By taxi
→ From $25 (Midway)–$45 (O'Hare) but from both airports it can take over one hour in heavy traffic

ACCESS TO AIRPORTS

• The following prices are for one double room en suite, based on the lowest rate in high season. They exclude breakfast and tax (15.4 percent)

• Booking via an Internet search engine or reservation agency such as the Chicago-based www.hotrooms.com can reduce prices significantly

• Most hotels offer complimentary wireless Internet, if not in every room, then in the lobby

UNDER $100

Hostelling International Chicago (A B3)
→ 24 E Congress Pkwy (State)
Tel. (312) 360-0300
www.hichicago.org
Clean, cheap hostel downtown. Some rooms en suite. $28–37, incl. breakfast. Add $3 if you haven't got Hostelling International membership.

Arlington House (C B4)
→ 616 W Arlington Pl. (Geneva); Tel. (773) 929-5380
www.arlingtonhouse.com
A hostel option close to the Lincoln Park nightlife, this is a popular spot for college-age travelers. Dorm and private rooms en suite available. $31–79.

Red Roof Inn (B C5)
→ 162 E Ontario St (Michigan)
Tel. (312) 787-3580
www.redroof.com
This solid, budget-friendly option may be nothing to write home about, but its location off Michigan Avenue, in the heart of downtown, is the draw. $83–159.

$100–$200

Days Inn Lincoln Park North (C B4)
→ 644 W Diversey Pkwy (Clark); Tel. (773) 525-7010
www.daysinnchicago.net
This inn at the north end of Lincoln Park has plain decor but all the basics, comfortable rooms, and a great location. From $116, incl. breakfast.

Ohio House Motel (B A5)
→ 600 N LaSalle St (Ohio)
Tel. (312) 943-6000
www.ohiohousemotel.com
A good budget-friendly option close to the Loop that makes up for its lack of high-end perks with gritty charm at its old-school diner. $100–160.

Seneca Hotel & Suites (B C4)
→ 200 E Chestnut St (Mies van der Rohe); Tel. (312) 787-8900; www.senecahotel.com
This 146-room bargain is tucked away on a quiet street. Reasonable rates for quality rooms – a remarkable combination in this area. $109–370.

Ramada Lake Shore (F D1)
→ 4900 S Lake Shore Dr.
Tel. (773) 288-5800
www.ramada-chicago.com
If you'd prefer to stay on the south lakeshore, where affordable rates still get you views of the lake, this is a good spot. There are free shuttles to downtown. From $119.

Wicker Park Inn (D B1)
→ 1329 N Wicker Park Ave
Tel. (773) 486-2743
www.wickerparkinn.com
One of the best places in Wicker Park, this five-room B&B has two self-contained apartments across the tree-lined street. From $129, incl. breakfast.

Gold Coast Guest House (B B3)
→ 113 W Elm St (Clark)
Tel. (312) 337-0361
www.bbchicago.com
On the edge of downtown, this B&B in an 1873 town house is known for its hospitality. It has a 20-ft-high window wall on a private garden and four rooms en suite; the Clark-

Transportation in Chicago

PURPLE LINE continues downtown weekday rush periods

Skokie 🅿&

YELLOW LINE

O'Hare ⬆
Rosemont 🅿&
Cumberland 🅿&
Harlem 🅿&

&Jefferson Park

BLUE LINE

Montrose
Irving Park
Addison
Belmont

&Logan Square
California
&Western

BROWN LINE

Kimball 🅿&
Kedzie &
Francisco &
Rockwell &
Western &
Damen ⊘

&Montrose
Irving Park ⊘
&Addison

Damen
Division
Chicago

Harlem/Lake &
Oak Park
Ridgeland
Austin
Central &
Laramie &
Cicero &
Pulaski &
Conservatory–Central Park &
Kedzie &

GREEN LINE

Forest Park 🅿&
Harlem
Oak Park
Austin
Cicero
Pulaski
Kedzie-Homan
&California
Western
Illinois Medical District&

BLUE LINE

&Polk
&18th

PINK LINE
54th/Cermak 🅿&
&Cicero
&Kostner
&Pulaski
&Central Park
&Kedzie
&California
&Western
&Damen

🅿&Kedzie

Pulaski 🅿&
Western 🅿&
Midway 🅿&

NORTH

ⓣ Free connection
    between routes

& Accessible station

🅿 Park & Ride Lot

⊘ Stations temporarily
⊘ closed for construction

▓▓▓▓ Rush periods only

chicago transit authority
www.transitchicago.com

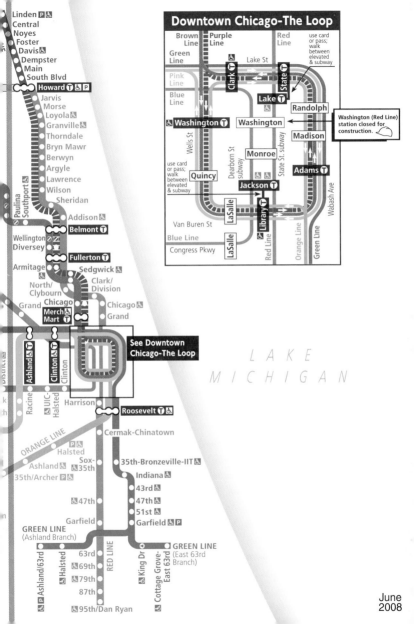

Downtown Chicago-The Loop

Washington (Red Line) station closed for construction.

June
2008

PUBLIC TRANSPORTATION

Chicago Transit Authority (CTA)

→ Tel. (312) 836-7000
www.transitchicago.com
Chicago's public transportation system is very accessible. The CTA runs a network of eight underground and elevated (hence the name 'the El') **train lines**. It also operates a **bus system** whose coverage extends to the suburbs.

Timetables

The busiest train lines (Blue and Red) run 24/7; overnight or night owl service (1am–5am) operates on the others. It is the same for buses (some will run nonstop), but trains are usually preferable because of their reliability and speed.

Fare and tickets

→ Basic cash fare for bus and train is $2.
→ A transit card – either a Chicago Card or a disposable transit card – can be refilled at any station. Up to two transfers allowed within a two-hour window (valid for transfers between buses and trains).
→ Visitor passes
1, 2, 3, and 5-day passes ($5, $9, $12, $18).

Metra

→ www.metrarail.com
Metra operates commuter trains linking the city to the outer suburbs. The main Metra station downtown is Ogilvie, at 500 W Madison St.

EXCURSIONS

of any hotel in Chicago, it stands regally at the north end of Michigan Avenue. Everything about the Drake is a buttoned-down traditional brand of fancy. The high tea is fun. $285–365.

LUXURY HOTELS

Ritz-Carlton Chicago (B B4)

→ 160 E Pearson St (Michigan); Tel. (312) 266-1000; www.fourseasons.com/chicagorc
Luxurious contemporary-style rooms and suites. The stunning lobby with skylight and indoor fountain is great for people watching. The Café serves lunch and dinner, and you can have tea in the Greenhouse. Spa, indoor pool, and sun deck with views of the city. Prime location too, just off the Mag Mile. $345–545.

Four Seasons (B B4)

→ 120 E Delaware Pl. (Michigan); Tel. (312) 280-8800; www.fourseasons.com
Spectacular views from the recently redone 343 rooms and suites; trademark luxury and service. Seasons restaurant for fine dining, the Lounge for nightly music, and a celebrated spa and rooftop pool. $395–600.

Peninsula (B B4)

→ 108 E Superior St (Rush) Tel. (312) 337-2888
www.peninsula.com
Famous for its pampering, and where Hollywood stays. This hotel of 389 rooms and suites decorated in traditional style has a state-of-the-art spa and magnificent pool with terrace; restaurants: Avenues, Shanghai Terrace, and the popular Pierrot Café and wine bar. $550 up to $7,900 for the Peninsula Suite.

EXCURSIONS

Chicago Botanic Garden

→ 1000 Lake Cook Rd, Glencoe; 20 miles north of Chicago; by car: I-90/94, then US Route 41; by Metra train to Glencoe or Braeside, then trolley or bus 213; Daily 8am–sunset
www.chicago-botanic.org
A dazzling 385-acre park of woods, islands, and lakes, with 23 gardens and over 9,000 plant varieties. Highlights include the Rose Garden; the six 'rooms' of the romantic English walled garden; the collection of 184 bonsais; and the Japanese Garden on its three islands. Take the tram tour for a better overview of the grounds.

Indiana Dunes National Lakeshore

→ 38 miles south of Chicago; by car: I-90/94, then Highway 12, which runs parallel to the shore; by train from Millennium Park to Dune Park (www.nictd.com); dunes open 7am–dusk
www.nps.gov/idnu
Head toward the smoke-belching heavy industry of northwest Indiana, past the factories and steel mills, and reach one of the most beautiful stretches of natural parkland in the region by the Lake Michigan shoreline. Beaches, hiking trails, picnic areas, and nature preserves dot the area. If you continue all the way up the coast, you'll hit Mt Baldy, a 126-foot sand dune that offers a great view all the way back to Chicago.

TRAVELING FROM CHICAGO BY TRAIN

Union Station (E E1)
→ 210 S Canal St
Daily 6am–10pm (ticketing hours); www.amtrak.com
The hub of the nationwide rail system, Amtrak.

TRAVELING FROM CHICAGO BY BUS

Greyhound (E E1)
→ 630 W Harrison (Jefferson)
Tel. (312) 341-1235
www.greyhound.com
The well-known intercity bus company. Book by telephone or in person at the terminal.

THE LAKEFRONT BIKE PATH

BIKES

While you must keep your wits about you and wear a helmet, biking is one of the easiest, cheapest, and best ways to get around. Many roads have separate cycle lanes and you can take your bike on CTA trains and buses outside peak hours. Biking along the scenic lakefront bike path is highly recommended whenever it's warm enough. The city's excellent website has rental information and maps of routes.
→ www.cityofchicago.org
And also:
→ www.chicagobikes.org

---

www.burnhamhotel.com
In 1895 architects Daniel Burnham, John Root, and Charles Atwood put up what was then the avant-garde glass-and-steel Reliance Building, now a boutique hotel of 122 rooms and suites done in a scheme of gold and blues. Prices fluctuate wildly, and a last-minute offer on the Internet can make this hotel affordable for many. Beaux Arts café, the Atwood. Unbeatable location; pet friendly. $219–359.

Sofitel Chicago Water Tower (B B4)
→ 20 E Chestnut St (Wabash)
Tel. (312) 324-4000
www.sofitel.com
Stylish vibe, stylish clientele. More interesting building than your average hotel, compliments of French architect Jean-Paul Viguier. $225–310.

Swissotel (B C6)
→ 323 E Wacker Dr.
Tel. (312) 565-0565
www.chicago.swissotel.com
If you want great views of the lake and the mouth of the Chicago River, this mirrored-glass tower is for you. It also has a very popular restaurant, the Palm. $229–299.

Wheeler Mansion (A C6)
→ 2020 S Calumet Ave (Cullerton); Tel. (312) 945-2020
www.wheelermansion.com
This historic 1870 mansion of 11 rooms and suites (the latter with fireplaces) has an old-fashioned, intimate feel. Bicycle rental available; garden terrace; $230–365, incl. breakfast.

Hotel InterContinental (B C5)
→ 505 N Michigan Ave (Illinois); Tel. (312) 944-4100
www.icchicagohotel.com
This Michigan Avenue landmark of 790 rooms and suites in modern and classic style has a junior Olympic-size swimming pool, 24-hour room service and business center, and two dining options: Zest and the Bar. $230–329.

Allegro (A A2)
→ 171 W Randolph St (LaSalle); Tel. (312) 236-0123
www.allegrochicago.com
A block from City Hall, this chic, recently restored historic hotel of 483 modern and stylish rooms has flat-screen TVs, Aveda products in the bathroom, and in-room spa services. $239–519.

W Chicago Lakeshore (B D5)
→ 644 N Lake Shore Dr. (Ontario); Tel. (312) 943-9200
www.whotels.com
This former Holiday Inn, redone in trendy W style, is right on the lake, with a beach next door; Bliss Chicago spa and a Rande Gerber-owned nightclub on the 33rd floor. Expect excellent views. 520 rooms. $249–395.

The Raffaello (B C4)
→ 201 E Delaware Pl. (Mies van der Rohe)
Tel. (312) 943-5000
www.chicagoraffaello.com
This is a trendy, organic-spa-style remake of a historic hotel. If you want your hotel to have a hydroponic garden on the roof – look no farther. $249–345.

Palmer House Hilton (A B2)
→ 17 E Monroe St (State)
Tel. (312) 726-7500
www.hilton.com
When the famous Potter Palmer built this hotel in 1873, it was notable for brand-new advances like electric lighting. Today, its main attraction is perhaps its opulent and historic lobby. $279–379.

Drake (B C3)
→ 140 E Walton St (Michigan)
Tel. (312) 787-2200
www.thedrakehotel.com
Arguably the best location

Street names, monuments, and places to visit are listed alphabetically. They are followed by a map reference, of which the initial letter(s) in bold (**A**, **B**, **C**...) relate to the matching map(s) within this guide.